Gustavus Woodson Smith

The Battle Of Seven Pines

Gustavus Woodson Smith

The Battle Of Seven Pines

ISBN/EAN: 9783744653428

Printed in Europe, USA, Canada, Australia, Japan

Cover: Foto ©ninafisch / pixelio.de

More available books at **www.hansebooks.com**

THE
BATTLE OF SEVEN PINES.

BY

GUSTAVUS W. SMITH,

FORMERLY MAJOR-GENERAL, CONFEDERATE STATES ARMY.

NEW YORK:
C. G. CRAWFORD, PRINTER AND STATIONER.
NOS. 49 AND 51 PARK PLACE.

1891.

PREFACE.

MANY of the published accounts of the battle of Seven Pines are about as dark and confusing as were the tangled woods and swamps in which most of the close and bloody fighting took place. The following quotations will illustrate the conflict of statements on this subject. Federal writers say: "It is hardly denied by the most passionate of McClellan's partisans that the way was open before him to Richmond on the afternoon of the first day; that being McClellan's greatest opportunity." "The Confederates had thrown almost their whole force against McClellan's left wing (Keyes and Heintzelman), and on the second day were streaming back to Richmond in discouragement and disorder." "We now know the state of disorganization and dismay in which the rebel army retreated." On the Confederate side it is stated: "The way to Richmond was not open to McClellan." "The first day the Confederates attacked McClellan's left wing with but five brigades." "So far from streaming back to Richmond in discouragement and disorder, they [the attacking party] remained in possession of the captured works on the Williamsburg road, nearly twenty-four hours after the fighting ended; and, on the Nine-miles road the Confederates closely confronted Sumner's corps at Fair Oaks for several days thereafter."

The above quotations are from the *Century Magazine* for January, 1889, page 477. They are referred to here as constituting one of "a thousand" instances of conflicting opinions in regard to the principal features of this battle—which seem to call for the publication of an accurate account of the main facts and the proofs. While endeavoring to prepare such an account I have felt constrained—at the risk of being tedious—to comment upon erroneous "assertions" of "high authorities;" and to give, in some detail, important evidence contained in the recently published official reports of regimental, brigade and division commanders, on both sides.

CONTENTS.

	PAGE.
Preliminary chapter........	7
Chapter II.—Fighting on the Williamsburg road, May 31.	34
Chapter III.—Alleged "slow movements" of Huger's division............	64
Chapter IV.—Contest north of Fair Oaks Station.	83
Chapter V.—The fighting, June 1........	105
Chapter VI.—Longstreet in the field, June 1.—D. H. Hill's official report.—Withdrawal of the Confederates from the captured works, June 2..........	127
Chapter VII.—Summary and comments.........	144
Fac-similes of letters...	174
Memoranda in reference to maps........	188
Preliminary map........	189
Map of battle-field........	191
Index.......	193

BATTLE OF SEVEN PINES.

PRELIMINARY CHAPTER.

In the latter part of May, 1862, the Army of Northern Virginia, about 50,000 strong, under General J. E. Johnston, reached the vicinity of Richmond from the defensive lines near Yorktown, and was followed by the army of the Potomac, nearly 100,000 strong, under General G. B. McClellan. There was a collision between the rear of the Confederates and the Federal advanced troops at Williamsburg, and a slight affair near the head of York river. Otherwise the withdrawal was not interfered with.

In retiring from Williamsburg, General J. E. Johnston's army was organized in two grand divisions, known as the First and Second Corps. The latter was commanded by Major-General James Longstreet and consisted of his own division and that of Major-General D. H. Hill. I commanded the First Corps, which was composed of the forces that were under Major-General J. B. Magruder, at Yorktown, before Johnston's army arrived there, and five other brigades; three of which, viz., Whiting's, Hood's and Hampton's, constituted a division under Brigadier-General Whiting; and the brigades of Pettigrew and Hatton, each of which reported direct to the headquarters of the First Corps. On the 28th of May, under authority from General Johnston, the following order was issued by my direction:

"The division now commanded by Brigadier-General Whiting and the brigades of Brigadier-General Pettigrew and Brigadier-General Hatton will, until further orders, constitute one division under command of Brigadier-General Whiting."

On the same day General Magruder was ordered to report direct to the headquarters of the army, and was thus transferred from my command. A. P. Hill's division was placed under my control, and the army was organized in three grand divisions. The "right wing," commanded by General Longstreet, was composed of his own division and that of D. H. Hill. The "centre," commanded by General Magruder, was composed of McLaws's division and that of D. R. Jones; and the "left wing," commanded by General G. W. Smith, was composed of my division, under Whiting, and A. P. Hill's division.

Such was the organization of the Confederate Army, near Richmond, when the following letter was written by General Johnston to General Whiting:

* "HEADQUARTERS, HARRISON'S,
"May 29th, 1862.

"*My Dear General:*

"I have just received the note you wrote in regard to your camp. I will give precise orders not to let it be interfered with. I received a message from Huger to the effect that his troops had not arrived at 6 hours 30 minutes this morning—no cars having been sent for them. The Quartermaster who had charge of the matter reported to me at sunset that the trains were ready and would be off at 9 o'clock. Lee ordered John G. Walker's brigade to Petersburg, and Holmes ordered it back.

"For any purpose but that contemplated yesterday the present disposition of our troops is not good—too strong on the extreme left. If nothing is heard of McDowell we must bring you back to a more central place.

"D. H. Hill reported an hour ago that one of his advanced brigadiers had sent forward 200 skirmishers, who very soon met a brigade of the enemy with cavalry and artillery. Who knows but that in the course of the morning Longstreet's scheme may accomplish itself.

"If we get into a fight here you'll have to hurry to help us.

"I think it will be best for A. P. H.'s troops to watch the

---

* A *fac-simile* of that letter is given on pages 174–5.

bridges and for yours to be well in this direction—ready to act anywhere. Tell G. W.*

"Yours truly,
"J. E. JOHNSTON.

"Brig.-Genl. Whiting."

In this connection the following extracts from ex-President Davis's writings are of interest. In a work entitled "The Rise and Fall of the Confederate Government," Vol. II., p. 120, he says: "Seeing no preparation to keep the enemy at a distance, and kept in ignorance of any plan for such purpose, I sent for General R. E. Lee, then at Richmond, in general charge of army operations, and told him why and how I was dissatisfied with the condition of affairs. . . . He then said: 'General Johnston should, of course, advise you of what he expects or proposes to do. Let me go and see him and defer this discussion until I return.' When General Lee came back, he told me that General Johnston proposed, on the next Thursday [May 29th], to move against the enemy as follows: General A. P. Hill was to move down on the right flank and rear of the enemy. General G. W. Smith, as soon as Hill's guns opened, was to cross the Chickahominy† at the Meadow Bridge, attack the enemy in flank, and by the conjunction of the two it was expected to double him up. Then Longstreet was to cross on the Mechanicsville Bridge and attack him in front. . . . On the morning of the day proposed I hastily dispatched my office business and rode out toward the Meadow Bridge to see the action commence."

Before giving Mr. Davis's account of the ride he makes "historic;" it may be well to call attention to the fact that—whatever may have been at one time General Johnston's contemplated purpose—on the morning of the 29th he certainly did not intend to attack the enemy that day. From this it follows that when Mr. Davis "rode out" that morning it was not likely he would "see the action commence."

---

* General G. W. Smith.

† That stream, at ordinary stages of water, is from forty to sixty feet wide and from two to three feet deep; in time of freshet it rises rapidly, overflows the low lands to a depth of several feet, and becomes a very serious military obstacle, passable only at the bridges.

In describing this remarkable ride he says: "On the road I found Smith's division halted and the men dispersed in the woods. . . . I finally saw General Hood, and asked him the meaning of what I saw. He told me he did not know anything more than that they had been halted. I asked him where General Smith was; he said he believed he had gone to a farm-house in the rear, adding that he thought he was ill. Riding on to the bluff which overlooks the Meadow Bridge, I asked Colonel [G. T.] Anderson, posted there in observation, whether he had seen anything of the enemy in his front. He said that he had seen only two mounted men across the bridge, and a small party of infantry on the other side of the river, some distance below, both of whom, he said, he could show me if I would go with him into the garden back of the house. There, by the use of a powerful glass, were distinctly visible two cavalry vedettes at the farther end of the bridge, and a squad of infantry lower down the river, who had covered themselves with a screen of green boughs. The Colonel informed me that he had not heard Hill's guns; it was, therefore, supposed he had not advanced. I then rode down the bank of the river, followed by a cavalcade of sightseers, who, I suppose, had been attracted by the expectation of a battle. The little squad of infantry, about fifteen in number, as we approached, fled over the bridge, and were lost to sight. Near to the Mechanicsville Bridge I found General Howell Cobb. . . . He pointed out to me on the opposite side of the river the only enemy he had seen, and which was evidently a light battery. Riding on to the main road, which led to the Mechanicsville Bridge, I found General Longstreet, walking to and fro in an impatient, it might be said, fretful manner. Before speaking to him, he said his division had been under arms all day waiting for orders to advance, and that the day was now so far spent that he did not know what was the matter. I afterward learned from General Smith that he had received information from a citizen that the Beaver Dam creek presented an impassable barrier, and that he had thus fortunately been saved from disaster. Thus ended the offensive defensive programme from which Lee expected much and of which I was hopeful."

The proper "front of the enemy," on the north side of the Chickahominy, was parallel to that stream, and extended from the vicinity of the railroad bridge on the left to Beaver Dam creek. But the right of their main line extended some distance along the east side of this creek, nearly at right angles to the Chickahominy. Thus, in order to move down on the *rear* of the enemy, as stated by Mr. Davis, A. P. Hill would have been compelled to make a wide detour to the north. Whilst G. W. Smith, according to Mr. Davis's account, would have struck the *front* of the line along Beaver Dam creek, and not as he says, "attacking the enemy *in flank*." By crossing "on the Mechanicsville Bridge" Longstreet—from Mr. Davis's description—would have been in rear of G. W. Smith. From that position he could not well have attacked the front of the Federal main line. General Johnston, as will presently be shown, did not propose to make the movements described by Mr. Davis.

Without commenting on his efforts to find out "where General Smith was"—and not doubting that Mr. Davis went "back of the house"—and without calling in question his statement that he, "followed by a cavalcade of sightseers," frightened a "little squad of infantry, about fifteen in number"—and finally found General Longstreet, who said "he did not know what was the matter"—I feel constrained to say that Mr. Davis never learned from me that I had received information from a citizen that the Beaver Dam creek presented an impassable barrier and that I "had thus fortunately been saved from disaster."

His account of the ride he took out on the Meadow Bridge road, after dispatching his office business on the morning of May 29, 1862, can only be fairly appreciated when viewed in the light of events as they occurred during the time of which he writes. Reference to those events will now be made.

On the 24th of May, Brigadier-General Hatton reported to me from Seven Pines : * "I will retire my command to-night to a point on the Seven-miles [Williamsburg Old Stage] road, one and a half miles from this. The enemy are in considerable force in my immediate front. In my skirmish to-day I lost but three men."

---

* The junction of the Williamsburg and the Nine-miles roads.

The same night it was reported to me that the bridges over the Chickahominy, including the Meadow Bridges, were in the hands of the enemy.

At that time D. H. Hill's division was on the Charles City road, three or four miles from Richmond; and Longstreet's division, on the extreme right, was at a little greater distance from the city, on the road leading to the James river defenses. Magruder's forces were on the Chickahominy bluffs, extending from the Meadow Bridge road to the New Bridge road, and along the latter to its junction with the Nine-miles road. The three brigades under Whiting, and the brigade of Pettigrew, were two or three miles from Richmond, between the left of D. H. Hill's division and the right of Magruder's forces. Hatton's brigade was farther out, watching the approach of the Federals on the Williamsburg road. There was no material change in the position of the Confederates until the 27th of May. That morning General McLaws reported that the Federal skirmishers were pressing ours on the Nine-miles road, just east of the New Bridge fork.

From the time the Federal advance first crossed the Chickahominy, at Bottom's Bridge, General Johnston had closely observed their movements, and was only waiting their approach within easy reach of his army, in order to strike them an effective blow. The report received from McLaws on the morning of the 27th gave strong indication that the enemy would soon be near enough, in large force, on either the Nine-miles road or the Williamsburg road, or on both, to bring them within good striking distance of Johnston's army.

But, attention was quickly called to McClellan's right flank, north of Richmond, across the Chickahominy, in the neighborhood of Mechanicsville. About 1 P. M. that day I received the following note from General Johnston:

* "Harrison's,
"May 27th, 1862.

"*Gustavus:*

"We must get ready to fight. Anderson reports (Junction, 11 A. M.) that his vedettes have informed him that McDowell is

---

* A *fac-simile* of this note is given on p. 176.

advancing 'in force,' his pickets at Guinea's. The army reported six miles this side of Fredericksburg.

"His main force at Half Sink, three regiments, under Hamilton, at the Junction. We must get ready for this.

"Yours ever,
"J. E. JOHNSTON.

"Major-Genl. SMITH."

Within fifteen minutes after I received the above note I was at General Johnston's headquarters. He directed me to order the five brigades from the Williamsburg road to the vicinity of Meadow Bridge; bring in A. P. Hill's division from the vicinity of Ashland; and make preparations for an attack upon the right of the Federal forces, on the left bank of the Chickahominy, as soon as possible. He told me that D. H. Hill's division would replace my troops on the Williamsburg road; and that Longstreet's division would be ordered to take position on the north and east of Richmond, ready to act in either direction. At my request I was relieved from the duty of commanding General Magruder and his forces; but the two brigades that formed D. R. Jones's division—the left of Magruder's line—on the Mechanicsville and Meadow Bridge roads, were left under my control, in the contemplated attack. At the same time it was arranged that Whiting should be placed in temporary command of the brigades of Pettigrew and Hatton in addition to the three brigades that had previously constituted his division.

In less than an hour from the time of my arrival at General Johnston's headquarters I left him for the purpose of making the requisite preparation to carry his instructions into effect. I returned about sunset, May 28th, and reported to him that A. P. Hill's division would be close in front of the Federal intrenched outpost at Mechanicsville, on the north side of the Chickahominy, before midnight, with orders to attack that place at dawn on the 29th; and that as soon as A. P. Hill's attack commenced, the division under Whiting, and D. R. Jones's division, would cross the Meadow and Mechanicsville bridges; and these three divisions, constituting the new left wing, under my command, would make a prompt and combined attack against the right of the Federal army, strongly posted on the eastern crest of Beaver Dam creek.

During the time that General Johnston's army was halted between the Pamunkey and Chickahominy rivers, a close reconnaissance of that ground, to include Beaver Dam creek, had been made by the Chief-Engineer of the Army, Major Stevens and the Chief of my Staff, Major Whiting; and these two officers had made to me a detailed report of their observations. I had, therefore, no occasion to listen to any citizen in regard to the character of the ground along Beaver Dam creek. I knew the difficulties we would have to encounter in a direct attack on that position. But, I advised that it should be attacked in front; because, in order "to turn it," we would have to make a wide movement far to the north, which would consume more time than we could afford, in our attempt to beat McClellan before McDowell could arrive.

The advantage that would accrue to us in turning the position —instead of attacking it in front—was clear to all; and suggestions were freely offered to the effect that, if Jackson's forces could be brought into position to turn the Federal line on Beaver Dam creek, and thus enable us to carry it without attacking in front, the matter would be much easier.

In short, I reported to General Johnston that I was satisfied the three divisions could carry the works at Beaver Dam creek by open assault in front; but, it would be a bloody business, called for, however, by the necessity for prompt action if we expected to beat McClellan before he was joined by McDowell.

After receiving my report General Johnston said that his latest information showed McDowell's army had returned to Fredericksburg; and it was believed he was moving north from that place. In this state of affairs there seemed to be no longer a pressing necessity for crossing the Chickahominy—all of whose bridges and fords were in the hands of the enemy—in order to attack the three Federal corps on the north side of that stream; first moving against the very strong position at Beaver Dam creek; while there were but two Federal corps on our side, and these were gradually coming within good striking distance, where the natural features of the ground were not against us.

But, General Longstreet urgently insisted that the contemplated attack should be made. Finally, General Johnston ordered that the attack should be suspended, and directed me to withdraw A. P. Hill's division, bring it to our side of the Chickahominy; and place it on the extreme left of the main Confederate Army. General Longstreet then proposed that an attack should be made early on the morning of the 29th, against the Federals, on our side of the river, in the vicinity of Seven Pines. General Johnston said it was not quite certain that McDowell had moved north from Fredericksburg; that the disposition of our troops, made whilst it was supposed McDowell was coming, was too strong on the left to admit of immediate and advantageous attack in the direction of Seven Pines; that Huger's division from Norfolk was expected to join us very soon; and that he was not yet fully assured the enemy east of us had approached near enough, in force worth crushing, to justify the engagement of the mass of our army in the swamps around Seven Pines, whilst the Federals were in position threatening the city upon the north side. No orders were given by General Johnston to attack on the 29th, but it was distinctly understood he would revert to his former intention, and endeavor to strike a sudden, and, if possible, crushing blow against the Federals in the vicinity of Seven Pines, if McDowell did not promptly come on.

I left General Johnston's headquarters about midnight on the 28th and remained at Colonel G. T. Anderson's position, near the Meadow Bridge, until I learned, early on the morning of the 29th, that A. P. Hill had received my order in time to enable him to withdraw, from close contact with the enemy at Mechanicsville, without his presence there having been discovered. The only crossing of the Chickahominy available for A. P. Hill's troops was the bridge on the road from Richmond to Ashland. I met him at that bridge and placed his command in position, on the left of the Confederate Army, as ordered by General Johnston.

Whilst I was thus engaged, it seems that President Davis was riding out on the Meadow Bridge road "to see the action commence;" and General Johnston was writing to D. H. Hill, on the Williamsburg road: "Tell your advanced brigades to find out the strength of the enemy before them, if possible. It may become necessary to attack." And later, on the same day, General Johnston wrote to General Whiting: " For any purpose but that contemplated yesterday, the present disposition of our troops is not good—too strong on the extreme left. . . . I think it will be best for A. P. H.'s troops to watch the bridges, and for yours to be well in this direction, ready to act anywhere."

In view of the plain facts, it is not necessary to say anything farther in regard to Mr. Davis's account of the ride he took, on the 29th of May, to see the action commence on the north side of the Chickahominy.

On the 30th, in compliance with the suggestions contained in General Johnston's letter of the 29th to General Whiting, I ordered the latter to take position nearer Richmond, and directed A. P. Hill to place his troops within easy supporting distance of those guarding the roads leading to the Meadow and Mechanicsville bridges. Huger's division, three brigades, from Norfolk, had arrived and was placed on the banks of Gilliss creek, near the eastern suburb of Richmond. D. H. Hill's division was still on the Williamsburg road, two or three miles from Richmond, with one brigade on the Charles City road farther out. Three brigades of Longstreet's division were a little north of the city, between the Mechanicsville and the Nine-miles roads, and the other three brigades of this division were three and one-half miles out on the latter road. After the divisions of A. P. Hill and Huger joined the Confederate forces near Richmond, General Johnston's army was between 60,000 and 70,000 strong.

Attention will now be called to a "programme" from which General Johnston "expected much," and of which, in the beginning, he was very "hopeful." On the 19th of December, 1867, he wrote to me: " The accounts of Federal officers of our operations in 1862 have revived an intention that I formed at the close of the war to make a military report. To assist me in doing so I ask your evidence on two points in which you are no less interested than myself."

The first point referred to by him was the conference held at Richmond, in April, 1862. The second was in reference to Seven Pines. On the 23d of the same month I replied, giving in substance, as requested, a description of what occurred on the Confederate side, north of Fair Oaks, late in the afternoon of the 31st of May, 1862, and gave him my recollections in regard to the Richmond conference. I added: "There is a good deal yet to be told before the world will understand what occurred at Seven Pines or Fair Oaks. Have you ever seen the 'History of the Army of the Potomac' (Federal) by Swinton? He attributes to my slowness—or worse—the failure of your plans; and leaves the impression that his narrative of events, on the Confederate side, was obtained from yourself and General Longstreet. When you requested me to omit certain facts, stated in my hurried official report to you, because, in your opinion, they did not concern me or my command, I acceded to the earnest request of a friend, and directed the paragraphs indicated, in pencil, by you, to be omitted. And 'History' now says (see Swinton's 'Army of the Potomac,' p. 135): 'Meantime, though the divisions of Longstreet and Hill had thus for three hours been vigorously pushing forward on the Williamsburg road, the column of G. W. Smith, to which had been intrusted the important flanking operation already indicated in Johnston's original plan, had not yet moved.' And a good deal more of the same sort of 'History' about the battle of Seven Pines. . . . I have always regretted that the serious attack of illness which I suffered from on the 2d of June (the day after Lee relieved me—and from which I have never fully recovered) prevented my requiring all subordinates to make full reports to me of what transpired during the eighteen hours I commanded on that battle field. . . . I am 'interested,' and I want all the facts known."

On the 16th of January, 1868, General Johnston replied: "I thank you for your explanation of the incident in the battle of Fair Oaks, which is so magnified by General Sumner and Mr. Swinton. I regard the passage of Mr. Swinton's book which you quote, and the next passage, as representing me (and truly) as fixing the time when your troops were put in motion. I think that examination of the two passages in connection will bring you to the same conclusion."

I replied on the 19th of the same month: "The question in reference to Swinton's account of the battle of Seven Pines, quoted in my letter of the 23d ult., is not as to whether you put my troops in motion at a given time, but in reference to slowness of G. W. Smith in carrying out your 'original plan.'"

General Johnston replied on the 21st of the same month, but confined his remarks exclusively to the first of the two points referred to in his letter of the 19th of December. He made no allusion to his "original plan," to Swinton's History, or to the battle of Seven Pines.

On page 133 of that "History" Mr. Swinton says: "Huger's duty was to strike the left flank of the Union force which Hill and Longstreet should engage in front." "G. W. Smith, with his division, was to advance on the right flank of the Union force which Hill and Longstreet should engage in front."

This is the alleged "original plan" to which, in a correspondence initiated by himself, I pointedly called General Johnston's attention, and which he studiously ignored. It is not proposed, in this connection, to discuss that part of the so-called "original plan" which refers to "Huger's duty."

The division which bore my name was not ordered "to advance on the right flank of the Union force which Hill and Longstreet should engage in front." The following is a copy of the order on this subject which was sent by General Johnston to General Whiting *direct*, although that order was at the same time sent to me. It is dated "May 30, 1862, 9.15 P. M.": "General—If nothing prevents, we will fall upon the enemy in front of Major-General [D. H.] Hill, who occupies the position on the Williamsburg road from which your troops moved to the neighborhood of Meadow Bridges, early in the morning, as early as practicable. The Chickahominy will be high—and passable only at the bridges—a great advantage to us. Please be ready to move by the Nine-miles road, coming as early as possible to the point at which the road to New Bridge turns off. Should there be cause of haste, General McLaws, on your approach, will be ordered to leave his ground for you, that he may reinforce General Longstreet."

It is now proposed to show what General Johnston's plan was, so far as concerned the movements of Longstreet's division and those of the division under Whiting. The head of the latter division, whilst moving to the Nine-miles road, very early on the morning of May 31, was obstructed in its progress by troops of Longstreet's division across its line of march. Becoming impatient at the continued delay, in his reaching the point at which the Nine-miles road leaves the suburb of the city, General Whiting addressed a note to General Johnston on that subject. The following is a copy of the reply he received from an Assistant Adjutant-General on Johnston's staff:

"General Johnston directs me to say, in answer to yours of this date, that Longstreet will precede you. What he said about McLaws [in the order for battle sent to Whiting] was merely in case of emergency. He has given no orders to Magruder." *

General Johnston intended that Longstreet's division should move along the Nine-miles road. Of this fact there is ample proof in the following letter written by General Johnston to me, within less than one month after the occurrence of these events:

†" RICHMOND,
"June 28, 1862.

" *My Dear Gustavus:*

"I inclose herewith the first three sheets of your report, to ask a modification, or omission, rather. They contain two subjects which I never intended to make generally known, which I have mentioned to no one but yourself, and mentioned to you as I have been in the habit of doing everything of interest in the military way. I refer to the mention of the misunderstanding between Longstreet and myself in regard to the direction of his division, and that of his note to me, received about 4 o'clock, complaining of my slowness, which note I showed you.

"As it seems to me that both of these matters concern Longstreet and myself alone, I have no hesitation in asking you to strike them out of your report, as they in no manner concern your operations.

"I received information of L.'s misunderstanding (which may be my fault, as I told you at the time), while his troops were moving to the Williamsburg road and sent to L. to send three

---

* Official Records, Vol. XI., Part III., p. 564.
† A *fac-simile* of that portion of this letter, which refers to operations at Seven Pines, is given on pages 177, 178.

brigades by the Nine-miles road, if they had not marched so far as to make the change involve a serious loss of time. This after telling you of the misunderstanding.

"Your march from Gen'l Semmes' headquarters was not in consequence of the letter from L. [Major] Whiting had gone at my request and with your permission to ascertain the state of things with L. Just before 4 o'clock we heard musketry for the first time, and [General] Whiting was ordered to advance. Just then Major W. rode up and reported from L. and a moment after the note was brought me, which, after reading it, I showed to you. . . ."

In those portions of this letter which are not quoted General Johnston makes no mention of operations connected with the battle of Seven Pines.

The following is a copy of the first three sheets of my official report, which was addressed to the Adjutant-General of the Department of Northern Virginia. Those portions that are in italics, included in brackets, were omitted, as requested by General Johnston:

"RICHMOND, VA.,
"June 23, 1862.

"*Major:*

"On the 28th of May, by direction of General Johnston, I assumed command of the left wing of the army, and on the same day placed my own division temporarily under command of the Senior Brigadier-General, W. H. C. Whiting. At half-past 12 o'clock on the morning of the 31st of May, at my headquarters on the Brook turnpike, I received a note from General Johnston directing that my division should take position as soon as practicable upon the Nine-miles road, near the New Bridge fork, ready to support, if necessary, the divisions upon the right in an attack upon the enemy, which was to be made early in the morning. I was informed that, in case my division did not arrive in time, a portion of the troops composing the centre would be moved forward, and I was directed in that event to replace the troops, thus moved, by my division. [*On arriving at the headquarters of General Johnston, about sunrise, I learned from him that his intention was that General Longstreet's division should move by the Nine-miles road, that of General D. H. Hill by the Williamsburg*

Stage road, and General Huger's by the Charles City road. The enemy, it was understood, had already upon this side of the Chickahominy river a force variously estimated at from 20,000 to 40,000 men. The recent rains had materially increased the difficulty of crossing that stream; and notwithstanding the very bad condition of the roads over which we had to pass, and the boggy, swampy condition of the fields and woods through which our troops would have to operate, it was believed that an energetic attack, early in the morning, properly supported and followed up, would result in defeat to that portion of the enemy already upon this side, before the other portion of their army could cross the swollen river; either to reinforce their troops, or to attack the city in our rear. About 8 o'clock I directed Captain Beckham, Aide-de-Camp, to see General Longstreet on the Nine-miles road, and learn from him the state of affairs, and communicate to me all the information he could obtain in regard to the probable movements of the troops under General Longstreet, in order that I might understandingly give instructions to General Whiting, who had arrived with the head of the division near General Johnston's headquarters, having been for some time waiting for General Longstreet's troops to pass. In about an hour I learned by note from Captain Beckham that neither General Longstreet nor any portion of his command were on the Nine-miles road. This note was immediately shown to General Johnston, who dispatched his Aide-de-Camp, Lieutenant Washington, to General Longstreet with directions to turn his division into the Nine-miles road, provided it could be done without material loss of time. This message did not reach General Longstreet. General Johnston's intentions, as then explained to me, were that whilst General D. H. Hill's division was attacking the enemy's advanced position on the Williamsburg Stage road in front, General Huger's division, from the Charles City road, would attack the left flank, and General Longstreet's division would engage the enemy on Hill's left. An hour later Captain Beckham reported that he had found Longstreet's division on the Williamsburg road, halted, for the purpose of allowing General D. H. Hill's troops to file by; and soon after returned with information that General Hill's troops had passed, and that General Longstreet was making all *his dispositions to attack the enemy in conjunction with General Hill's division on the Williamsburg road, his own division being held in reserve on that road.*] I then directed General Whiting to move three brigades, viz., his own, Hood's and Pettigrew's, near to the fork of the Nine-miles and New Bridge roads; and placed the other two—Hatton's and Hampton's—in reserve near Mrs. Christian's farm. About 1 o'clock I rejoined General Johnston at the head of the three brigades in position upon the Nine-miles road, and found him anxiously awaiting the development of affairs upon our right. As the day wore on and nothing decisive was heard from General Longstreet's attack, except occasional firing of cannon, and, for some two or three hours, but little musketry, it seemed that no real attack was likely to be made that day, at least. [*But between 4 and 5 o'clock a note was received from General Longstreet stating that he had attacked and beaten the enemy after several hours severe fighting; that he had been disappointed in not receiving assistance upon his left, and, although it was now nearly too late, that an attack by the Nine-miles road upon the right flank and rear of the enemy would probably yet enable him to drive them into the Chickahominy before dark.*"]

The omissions indicated by General Johnston were made as shown in the preceding italics within brackets. I now have the first three sheets of my report as they were returned to me by him. He made a mistake in stating that he mentioned to no one but myself the misunderstanding between himself and Longstreet in regard to the direction in which the division of the latter was to move. He is mistaken, too, in supposing that this matter concerned himself and Longstreet alone, and that it " in no manner " concerned the operations of the division under Whiting.

The note he received at 4 P. M., complaining of his " slowness," gave him good reason to believe that, up to that time, the 30,000 men of the right wing had met with more resistance than their united efforts could well overcome; and the consequence was, that General Johnston, in person, led the division under Whiting in a rapid movement directed against "the right flank of Longstreet's adversaries;" without further regard to Federal reinforcements that would, in all probability, be sent from the north bank of the Chickahominy as soon as possible after Longstreet's attack commenced.

It was about 4.30 A. M., May 31, when I reached General Johnston's headquarters. I reported to him that before I left my own headquarters, five or six miles distant, General Whiting had informed me that in compliance with orders received direct from General Johnston, he would start with the head of the division as soon as it was light enough to see the road; and that he would be on time. I informed General Johnston that I had turned over the command of the left wing of the army temporarily to A. P. Hill; and although I purposed being on the field, I did not propose to relieve General Whiting from the command of my division, to which he had recently been assigned.

General Johnston approved of what I had done and proposed to do, and informed me of his intentions as stated in my report, including the portions that were omitted at his request. He told me that he would, in person, be on the Nine-miles road, from which he could better observe the movements of the Federals on the north side of the river; and stated that if they attempted to cross anywhere above New Bridge he would place me in command of all our troops on that side, and that I must repel any attack they might make on Richmond, whilst the mass of our army was engaged with McClellan's left wing.

At that time, General Johnston confidently expected an effective blow would be struck against the Federals in the vicinity of Seven Pines—before 8 A.M.—by D. H. Hill's division on the Williamsburg road, moving against their front, closely supported by Longstreet's division, on the Nine-miles road, going promptly into action on D. H. Hill's left.

But, Mr. Swinton says: "Johnston's original plan," was that "G. W. Smith, with his division, was to advance on the right flank of the Union force which Hill and Longstreet should engage in front"—and adds: "Meantime, though the divisions of Longstreet and Hill had thus for three hours been vigorously pushing forward on the Williamsburg road; the column of G. W. Smith, to which had been intrusted the important flanking operation already indicated in Johnston's original plan had not yet moved." This view has been so persistently insisted upon that some additional testimony bearing on the question of "Johnston's original plan" will now be given.

In a letter to me, February 7, 1863, Major R. F. Beckham, who was my aide at the time of this battle, says: "I was directed to carry an order [message] to General Longstreet urging him to push forward with his division so that the road might be cleared to enable your division [under Whiting] to take up the march. . . . I then asked General Johnston if he could give me any idea of General Longstreet's whereabouts. His reply was that he did not know, but that he ought to be on the march on the Nine-miles road. With instructions to find him, if possible, I started off; but could learn nothing of him on the route indicated by General Johnston. After having gone as far as was necessary to satisfy me that General Longstreet's division was not on the Nine-miles road, I sent, by courier, a note to you stating this fact; and I also remember to have said in it that I would go over to the Williamsburg, or old stage road, and see if General Longstreet could be found there. I found his headquarters at a house on the side of the road, belonging, I think, to a Mr. Poor, and there delivered to him the order [message] given me. Kemper's brigade, which formed a part of General Longstreet's division, was at a halt on the road when I got to General Longstreet's headquarters, and, what surprised me most, was accompanied by wagons loaded with baggage and camp equipage. You will remember that I mentioned this thing to you when I came back to General Johnston's headquarters. I do not remember at what hour I reached General Longstreet. Judging from the time of my joining you at General Johnston's, and the time which must have elapsed before the order [to deliver a message to General Longstreet] was given me, I would suppose it to have been about 10 o'clock when I reached Poor's house."

The following extracts are from a letter to me by Major S. B. French, who was Chief Commissary of my command. This letter was written soon after the publication of Mr. Swinton's History of the Army of the Potomac.

"In compliance with your request, I have the pleasure of furnishing you, to the best of my recollection, with incidents and facts associated with movements made on the 31st of May,

1862—the battle of Seven Pines. On the morning of that day, under your orders, I, with other members of your staff, followed you to the headquarters of General Johnston, known as the Stubbs House, and there learned, as an officer of your staff, particulars of movements preparatory to an attack upon the enemy's forces on the south side of the Chickahominy. General Longstreet had been ordered to move his own division on the Nine-miles road; General D. H. Hill on the Williamsburg, and General Huger on the Charles City—three divisions, forming the right wing of the army, under the command of General Longstreet. General Whiting, commanding your own proper division, had been ordered by General Johnston to move at an early hour to the Nine-miles road and act as a support to General Longstreet, who had been directed to engage the enemy. General Whiting, with his command, within a short distance of General Johnston's headquarters, reported that his march was impeded by the movement of General Longstreet's troops across his line of march, and in the direction of the Williamsburg road. With this information, you ordered Colonel Beckham, then Lieutenant and Aide-de-Camp, to go to General Longstreet and find out his exact position, and report to him the delay—in the movement of Whiting's command, caused by Longstreet's division crossing Whiting's line of march—and have it remedied. In about an hour after that a courier arrived from Lieutenant Beckham, stating that he could not find General Longstreet or his command, and was fully satisfied that neither he nor his division was on the Nine-miles road. General Johnston, on receipt of this information, and being satisfied that Beckham must be mistaken, dispatched his Aide-de-Camp, Lieutenant Washington, in search of General Longstreet on the Nine-miles road, which resulted in the capture of Washington. Colonel Beckham, on his return to headquarters, reported that General Longstreet was on the Williamsburg road, and the troops he saw had halted, having with them their baggage wagons, etc. Some time after Beckham returned, you, with a selection of officers of your staff, moved, under orders from General Johnston, to a point and with an object not known to me, leaving myself and a number of your officers to accompany General Johnston on the Nine-miles road, which we did, and remained with him until you rejoined us about half a mile this side of the junction of the New Bridge and Nine-miles roads. At the house selected for headquarters much anxiety was manifested because of the unaccountable delay of General Longstreet in striking the enemy. General Johnston requested me to listen for musketry, and when I reported that I could not hear any, he said that he wished the troops were back in their camps. Subsequently information was received at headquarters that Longstreet had engaged the enemy. I cannot remember the hour when this information arrived, but am inclined to think it was after 4 o'clock in the afternoon when General Johnston left his headquarters and galloped down the Nine-miles road to the point where General Whiting was in command of your division. You followed soon after General Johnston. When I arrived on the field General Johnston was, in person, giving orders for the movement of the troops under General Whiting, and called upon the different members of your staff to assist him, which they cheerfully did. I understood at the time of the fight, in fact prior to leaving General Johnston's headquarters (in the suburbs of Richmond), that you were on the field without an immediate command— though a portion of your troops under General Whiting were engaged—for the purpose of rendering any assistance occasion might demand, and watching the movements of the enemy. I do not remember now of your taking any active part in the affair until it was reported that General Hampton's command was in much peril, and unless assistance was rendered, it would possibly be crushed. This aid you promptly rendered, so far as it was in your power, and in person went immediately to the scene of action. I saw very little of you after that during the engagement; but was quite near General Johnston when he was wounded."

The following quotation is from a letter to me, dated Milledgeville, Ga., February, 1868, written by Colonel B. W. Frobel, of the Confederate States Engineers, who was a Major on General Whiting's staff at the battle of Seven Pines:

"You have called my attention to the account given by Mr. Swinton in his 'History of the Army of the Potomac' of this battle; Mr. Swinton is surely greatly mistaken. The division was under the immediate command of General Whiting, and he directly under General Johnston, who was with the division the whole day until he was wounded late in the afternoon. I am satisfied that no blame can attach to General Whiting for not being on the field sooner. Mr. Swinton must also be mistaken about the slowness of that division frustrating an important flank movement indicated in 'Johnston's original plan.' I never heard of the movement until I saw it mentioned in Mr. Swinton's book, and certainly no mention was made of it in any battle order sent to our headquarters."

I had taken no part in the planning of this battle; in fact knew nothing of it, in detail, until the morning of the 31st of May. I had no special command on the field; but I was there, and a large portion of my staff officers were with me. I was in the front line of the fighting north of Fair Oaks late that afternoon, but my proper command—the left wing of the army—was six or eight miles distant. Although I commanded the whole Confederate army from dark on the 31st of May, until I turned over the command to General Lee early in the afternoon of the 1st of June—before it was known the fighting had ended—I did not purpose making an official report; because I was suddenly taken very seriously ill on the morning of June 2d, and was immediately conveyed to Richmond; became steadily worse for two or three weeks, and was advised by my physicians that perfect quiet, mountain air, and the free use of sulphur waters, offered the only chance for my recovery. A short time before I was taken from Richmond to the mountains, General Johnston appealed to me to make to him a written report of the operations of my division up to the time he was disabled and removed from the field. In reply I stated that he knew the division was not then under my command; that he himself was with it, in person, from early in the morning, and directed its movements, until he was wounded, and that my health was such that I could not write. To this he replied: "You were with the division, although not in direct command; and you can dictate your report." Finally I yielded to his solicitations. Neither of us was on duty at that time. In making the report, I alluded to some of the incidents connected with my command of the army, on the 1st of June, but did not make a detailed statement of that day's operations.

In his official report, General Johnston says : " General Longstreet, being near my headquarters, received verbal instructions." "General Hill, supported by General Longstreet (who had the direction of operations on the right), was to advance by the Williamsburg road to attack the enemy in front." In that report he makes no allusion to the transfer of Longstreet's division to the Williamsburg road, and does not refer to his attempt to have three brigades of that division sent back to the Nine-miles road.

General Longstreet, in his official report, says nothing in regard to the transfer of his division from the Nine-miles road, and its vicinity, to the Williamsburg road, and gives no intimation that he received any orders prescribing the direction in which his division was to move into action.

Reference will now be made to the state of affairs on the Federal side. On the night of May 30, Keyes' corps was in the vicinity of Seven Pines ; Heintzelman's corps at Bottom's Bridge and White Oak Bridge ; both of these corps, on the south side of the Chickahominy, were under the control of General Heintzelman ; Sumner's corps was on the north side of the Chickahominy, between the Railroad Bridge and New Bridge ; and two corps were between Sumner and Mechanicsville. Besides the fortifications at Bottom's Bridge and White Oak Bridge there were three fortified " lines of defense " across the Williamsburg road. The first of these lines—five-eighths of a mile west of Seven Pines—was held by Casey's division of Keyes' corps. The second—at Seven Pines—was held by Couch's division of that corps. The third line of defense, about one and a half miles east of Seven Pines, was unoccupied. Kearney's division, of Heintzelman's corps, was at Bottom's Bridge ; and Hooker's division was at White Oak Bridge. A bridge across the Chickahominy had been constructed in front of each of the two divisions of Sumner's corps—Sedgwick's and Richardson's divisions.

Except the open ground immediately around the first and second lines of defense, the country generally in the immediate vicinity of Seven Pines was densely wooded. The ground was flat and swampy, the undergrowth tangled with matted vines-

Both of these lines were strengthened by rifle-pits which extended a short distance on each side of the road, with abatis or felled timber in front. In the first line there was a small unfinished pentangular redoubt just south of the Williamsburg road; and the abatis of the second line extended in a curve to the rear across the Nine-miles road. The left of both lines was protected by the almost impracticable White Oak Swamp; but the ground on the right offered no strong features for defense. Two regiments and a battery were detached and posted near Fair Oaks Station, to guard the depot of supplies at that place, where there were no artificial defenses. About 1,000 yards in front of the rifle-pits of the first line of defense, and nearly at right angles to the Williamsburg road, a skirmish line extended from the White Oak Swamp on the Federal left to the Chickahominy river. Two regiments were detached to support the right of the skirmish line—one south of the railroad and not far from it, the other on the Nine-miles road. On the morning of the 31st, the two divisions of Keyes' corps were in their camps just in rear of their respective rifle-pits, while strong working parties were engaged upon the unfinished earthworks and other artificial defenses.

On that morning General Keyes reported to General McClellan's chief of staff: "Everything on the part of the Confederates indicates an attack on my position, which is only tolerably strong, and my forces are too weak to defend it properly. Brigadier-General Sumner told me yesterday he should probably cross the Chickahominy last night. If he did so, and takes post nigh Old Tavern and this side, I should feel more secure than I do now."*

In his "Fifty Years' Observations," General Keyes says:

"The left of my lines was all protected by the White Oak Swamp, but the right was on ground so favorable to the approach of the enemy, and so far from the Chickahominy, that if Johnston had attacked there an hour or two earlier than he did, I could have made but a feeble defense comparatively, and every man of us would have been killed, captured, or driven into the swamp or river before assistance could have reached us."

---

* "Official Records," Vol. XI., Part III., page 203.

If Johnston's intentions in regard to the direction in which Longstreet's division should move into action had been carried into effect, and the attack had been made early in the morning, there can hardly be a reasonable doubt that Keyes's corps would have been destroyed before it could have been reinforced. His easily accessible right flank—the point at which attack was, and ought to have been, expected—should have been, as he indicates, strengthened by additional troops. Confederate success on that side would have cut the Federal army in two—separated its right wing from its left and exposed the latter to destruction.

Glancing now at the Confederate side, it will be borne in mind there are two main roads leading from Richmond to Seven Pines. One is the Nine-miles road which leads from the northeast suburb of the city, by Old Tavern and Fair Oaks Station to Seven Pines. The distance to the latter point by this road is nine miles, and from Fair Oaks Station to Seven Pines is something less than one mile. Three brigades of Longstreet's division, under the command of Brigadier-General Cadmus M. Wilcox, were on that road three and one-half miles from the city during the night of the 30th. And the other three brigades of Longstreet's division were north of the city, not far distant from the point at which the Nine-miles road leaves the suburbs.

The Williamsburg road leads from the southeast suburb of Richmond, and it is by this road seven miles from the city to Seven Pines. On the night of the 30th, three brigades of D. H. Hill's division were on this road, two or three miles from the city, and one brigade (Rodes's) was three or four miles out on the Charles City road, south of the White Oak Swamp. Huger's division was on Gilliss Creek, not far north of the point at which the Williamsburg road leaves the suburbs. General Johnston placed Longstreet in command of these three divisions, gave him "verbal instructions," and ordered that the movement should begin "at daybreak."

General Wilcox, in his official report, says that three brigades of Longstreet's division, under his command, were in camp near the "Mechanicsville" road during the night of the 30th. He tells me, however, that he had no map of the country, knew very little about the names of the roads, but distinctly remembers that his troops were three and one-half miles from the city, on a road that passed close to General Johnston's headquarters, near the northeast suburb of Richmond, and led to New Bridge; that is the Nine-miles road.

He says that at 6.30 A. M. these three brigades moved from their camps and proceeded " by by-paths across to the junction of the Charles City and Williamsburg roads, and remained at this point till 3.30 P. M."* If they had moved at dawn, say 3.30 A. M., they could easily have reached McLaws's line on the New Bridge road before 6 A. M., and would then have been in the position from which General Johnston intended Longstreet's division should move into action and closely support the attack D. H. Hill was to make against the Federals on the Williamsburg road.

The following quotation from a letter written by General R. E. Colston, who commanded one of the three brigades under Wilcox, bears directly upon the movements that morning. General Colston says: " A little brook [Gilliss Creek] near Richmond was greatly swollen, and a long time was wasted crossing it on an improvised bridge made of planks, a wagon mid-stream serving as a trestle. Over this the division [Longstreet's] passed in single file, you may imagine with what delay. If the division commander had given orders for the men to sling their cartridge-boxes, haversacks, etc., on their muskets and wade without breaking formation, they could have crossed by fours at least, with water up to their waists, . . . and hours would have been saved. . . . When we got across we received orders to halt on the roadside until Huger's division passed us. There we waited for five or six hours.

Some additional light is thrown upon this subject by the following extract from a letter written by Governor William E. Cameron, who was Adjutant of the Twelfth Virginia, of Mahone's brigade, Huger's division. Governor Cameron says:

" Longstreet [three brigades of his division] moved that morning from Fairfield racecourse, and arrived at the crossing of the [Gilliss] creek in front of the command [of Huger]. We waited till Longstreet cleared the way, crossed the creek about 10.30

---

* " Official Records," Vol. XI., Part I., page 986.

A. M., moved as far as the Tudor House, rested there until 1 P. M." Mahone's brigade then moved out on the Charles's City road; "the men were fresh, eager, and in light marching trim. The roads were bad, but there was no physical obstruction of any moment, and we met no enemy."

From what has already been stated, it is clearly seen that Longstreet's "misunderstanding," which resulted in the transfer of his division to the Williamsburg road, not only "concerned" the movements of the division under Whiting, but materially delayed Huger's division at the Gilliss Creek crossing. Longstreet, by authority from General Johnston, then assumed control of Huger's division. Delay on the part of the latter after that time must be attributed to General Longstreet, unless it can be shown that Huger did not obey Longstreet's orders.

Captain B. Sloan, of General Huger's staff, says: "Longstreet's brigades as they successively reached the plain above the creek halted and remained for an hour or two resting on their arms. This plain (in front of General Huger's headquarters) was, perhaps, between three and four miles in rear of the battle-field. Here, at a farm-house, Huger met Longstreet and [D. H.] Hill, and a discussion was had as to the relative rank of the division commanders. Longstreet claimed (by instructions from General Johnston) to be in command of that portion of the army. After protest Huger acquiesced." "It was then possibly 10 A. M. or 11 A. M." After that time "Huger's movements were directed by Longstreet."

After Longstreet took control of Huger, one brigade of the division of the latter was sent out on the Charles City road to the point at which Rodes's brigade of D. H. Hill's division had been in observation. Two brigades of Huger's, with three of Longstreet's, were retained near the junction of the Wiiliamsburg and Charles City roads until 3.30 P. M.; the disposition made of these five brigades, by General Longstreet, after that time, will be shown in another connection. It is enough now to say that these five brigades reached the front too late to be put into the fight that day.

Brigadier-General George E. Pickett, in his official report, says: "On the afternoon of May 31, and just as the battle of

Seven Pines was being opened by Major-General Longstreet, I was directed by that officer to move [from the Williamsburg road] with my brigade to the York River Railroad, cover the same, repel any advance of the enemy up that road, and to hold myself in readiness to move to the support of our advance if needed. About 9 P. M. received orders from General Longstreet to march my brigade at daylight [June 1] and report to Major-General D. H. Hill."

Two brigades of Longstreet's division followed after the four brigades of D. H. Hill's division when the latter, at 1 P. M., moved on the Williamsburg road to make the attack. But only one of those two brigades went into close action.

In the attempt to destroy Keyes's corps, early on the morning of May 31, General Johnston certainly did not intend that five brigades of Longstreet's division should be kept out of the fight during the whole of that day.

In his "Narrative," page 133, General Johnston says: "Longstreet . . . . was instructed, verbally, to form his own and Hill's division in two lines crossing the Williamsburg road at right angles, and to advance to the attack in that order." There is nothing to this effect in the official report of either General Johnston or General Longstreet. But, the statements made by General Johnston to me that day—and in his letter to me June 28, 1862—together with other evidence previously referred to, show, beyond question, that General Johnston intended Longstreet's division should move on the Nine-miles road, and be put in action on D. H. Hill's left. He certainly did not intend that Longstreet's division should be transferred from the Nine-miles road to the Williamsburg road. When he was informed that such transfer had been, or was being, made, he endeavored to have three brigades of that division sent back to the Nine-miles road, " if they had not advanced so far as to make the change involve a serious loss of time." Longstreet made no attempt to form his division in line of battle "crossing the Williamsburg road at right angles, and to advance to the attack."

CHAPTER II.

FIGHTING, ON THE WILLIAMSBURG ROAD, MAY 31.

Federal Accounts.—General Silas Casey, commanding the advanced division of Keyes's corps, says, in his official report: "I occupied with my division the advanced position of the army, about three-fourths of a mile [west] from the cross-roads at the Seven Pines, where I caused rifle pits and a redoubt to be thrown up; also an abatis to be commenced about one-third of a mile in front of the pits, and parties were employed upon these works on the morning of the 31st. . . . My pickets, . . . toward the right of my [skirmish] line, succeeded [about 10 A. M.] in capturing Lieutenant Washington, an aide of General Johnston. . . . This circumstance . . . led me to exercise increased vigilance. Between 11 and 12 o'clock a mounted vedette was sent in from the advanced pickets to report that a body of the enemy was in sight, approaching on the Richmond road. I immediately ordered the One Hundred and Third Regiment Pennsylvania Volunteers to advance to the front for the purpose of supporting the pickets. It was soon afterward reported to me by a mounted vedette that the enemy were advancing in force, and about the same time two shells were thrown over my camp. . . . [I] immediately ordered the division under arms, the men at work on the rifle-pits and abatis to be recalled and join their regiments, the artillery to be harnessed up at once, and made my dispositions to repel the enemy. While these were in progress the pickets commenced firing. I directed Spratt's battery of four pieces, 3-inch rifled guns, to advance [just north of the Williamsburg road] in front of the rifle pits about one-fourth of a mile. . . . [I] supported this battery by three regiments of Naglee's brigade and one of Palmer's."

General Casey then states in detail the preparations made for defense, and adds: "About fifteen minutes after these dispositions had been completed I directed the advanced battery to open. . . . In a short time" the regiment," which at the first alarm had been ordered to the support of the pickets, came down the road in some confusion, having suffered considerable loss. . . . The enemy now attacked me in large force on the centre and both wings. . . . In order to save" Spratt's battery, I " ordered a charge of bayonets by the four supporting regiments at the centre, which was executed in a most gallant and successful manner under the immediate direction of Brigadier-General Naglee. . . . When the charge had ceased, but not until the troops had reached the edge of the wood [west of the first abatis], the most terrible fire of musketry commenced that I have ever witnessed. The enemy again advanced in force, and the flanks being again severely threatened, a retreat to the works [the rifle-pits and the unfinished pentangular redoubt] became necessary. To be brief, the rifle-pits were retained until they were almost enveloped by the enemy. . . . The troops then retreated to the second line, in possession of General Couch's division."

"Under the circumstances I think it my duty to add a few remarks with regard to my division. On leaving Washington [a few weeks ago] eight of the regiments were composed of raw troops. It has been the misfortune of the division in marching through the Peninsula to be subjected to an ordeal which would have severely tried veteran troops. Furnished with scanty transportation, occupying sickly positions, exposed to the inclemency of the weather, at times without tents or blankets, and illy supplied with rations and medical stores, the loss from sickness has been great, especially with the officers. . . . Notwithstanding all these drawbacks, and the fact that there were not 5,000 men in line of battle, they withstood for three hours the attack of an overwhelming force of the enemy. . . . It is true that the division, after being nearly surrounded by the enemy and losing one-third of the number actually engaged, retreated to the second line. They would all have been prisoners of war had they delayed their retreat a few minutes longer."

This vindication of his division was called out by the following telegram, sent from the battlefield, by General McClellan to Secretary Stanton, on the 1st of June : " Casey's division, which was the first line, gave way unaccountably and discreditably. . . . With the exception of Casey's division our men behaved splendidly." That telegram did cruel injustice to Casey's division and was, perhaps, too complimentary to some of the other troops.

As already stated, Casey's division was encamped in rear of the earthworks of the Federal first line of defense, across the Williamsburg road, nearly at right angles to it, and five-eighths of a mile West of Seven Pines. It was composed of Naglee's brigade, five regiments, on the right; Wessells' brigade, four regiments, in the centre, across the road; and Palmer's brigade, four regiments, on the left. The latter two brigades were composed entirely of raw troops. Two of Naglee's regiments and some two or more companies were detached in support of the right of the picket line.

When the Confederate advance was reported, the One Hundred and Third Pennsylvania, of Wessells' brigade, was ordered forward on the Williamsburg road to support the pickets; two regiments of this brigade were placed in the rifle-pits, extending from the redoubt across the road, and one regiment was a short distance in advance of the rifle pits. General Wessells says the "actual strength [of his brigade] in action [was] less than 1,500 men."

General Palmer says that one of his regiments "was deployed in the field to the extreme left of our line and in front of the woods [south of the redoubt] through which the enemy made the flank movement;" one of his regiments was in the rifle-pits, immediately on the left of the redoubt, and two regiments "were ordered to the front and to the support of the batteries." "I estimate the whole fighting force [in this brigade] on the ground, at less than 1,000 officers and men."

Naglee's brigade was partly in support of Spratt's battery, partly in support of the picket line and partly on duty in the picket line. In his official report General Naglee says: "There were taken into action [in his brigade] eighty-four officers and 1,669 men." On these data the actual fighting force, of the three brigades which constituted Casey's division, was 4,253.

The commander of that regiment of Wessells' brigade which was ordered to support the pickets, says: "At about 1 o'clock P. M., . . . under orders from Brigadier-General Wessells', I marched my regiment out and formed it immediately in rear of the picket reserves and about half a mile from our camp. . . . When the pickets were fired on and driven in I ordered the reserve to take their places in the regiment. . . . The enemy's fire now opened along the whole line and we were also subjected to a very heavy cross fire from both flanks. . . . I ordered my men to fall back slowly, which they did, and formed on a road running nearly at right angles to the one on which we had entered the woods. The overwhelming force of the enemy, which now almost surrounded us, compelled me again to retire, to prevent being entirely cut off. Owing to the nature of the ground, which was marshy and covered with underwood and fallen timber, it was impossible to retire in order. The regiment when marched out consisted of 430 men."

General Wessells gives this regiment credit for having fought well, until driven from the woods "exposed to the terrific fire from the front and both flanks;" "followed by the enemy, who was [now] seen to emerge from the woods and advance."

After losing nearly one-fourth of its numbers, in a few minutes, the regiment seems to have broken to pieces whilst being hurled back through the abatis in front of Casey's riflepits. General Keyes says: It "broke shortly and retreated, joined by a great many sick. The numbers as they passed down the road as stragglers conveyed an exaggerated idea of surprise and defeat."

The real hard fighting now began; and there was a prolonged contest in the abatis in front of Spratt's battery. The bayonet charge referred to by General Casey is described in the official report of Colonel Davis in command of the One Hundred and Fourth Pennsylvania, of Naglee's brigade. He says: "The regiments sprang forward towards the enemy with a tremendous yell. . . . The battle now raged with great fury and the firing was much hotter than before. . . . The enemy being largely re-enforced, pressed us in front and flank. . . . We could not hold our position much longer unless re-enforced. . . . Receiving no re-enforcements, we were ordered with Spratt's battery to retire, but unfortunately, the horses of one of the pieces being killed, we were compelled to abandon that piece."

When the troops in front were withdrawn, they formed in the rifle-pits, and the contest continued hot along the whole of Casey's line. One regiment of Peck's brigade was sent forward, from the second line, in the woods south of the main road, by General Keyes; and the Fifty-fifth New York, of the same brigade, was directed to move on that road, led by General Naglee, to aid in protecting the heavy artillery in the unfinished redoubt. General Naglee says he placed that regiment "about fifty yards in advance of the redoubt, the left resting a short distance from the road." He adds: "Leaving the Fifty-fifth, my attention was directed toward the right, where I found the Fifty-sixth New York with the Eleventh Maine [of his own brigade that had been detached supporting the picket line] . . . had fallen back about 400 yards . . . and were again placed . . . about midway between the Williamsburg road and the railroad, and about 300 yards in front of the Nine-miles road. Near by I found the Fifty-second Pennsylvania. . . . At this time the fire here had considerably slackened, but was increasing on the left. . . . The enemy had discovered, what I had long feared, that there were none of our troops between the White Oak Swamp and a line parallel with and but 200 yards from the Williamsburg road. . . . At the time of my return [the Confederates] had driven our men from the rifle-pits," "being successful in turning our left flank." " The entire field in front of and including the redoubt being in possession of the enemy."

In falling back from their rifle pits and redoubt, Casey's forces, whilst moving across the abatis in front of Couch's rifle-pits, endeavored to make a stand. But their own guns, which they had lost, were turned upon them; this, added to the fire of the advancing Confederate infantry and artillery, hurled them back in great disorder through the second abatis; and a portion of Casey's troops, finding the short rifle-pits of Couch's line already occupied and overcrowded, continued their retreat.

In the meantime Naglee's regiments, that had been supporting the picket line on the right, retained the ground on which he had last placed them—in the woods, half way between the Williamsburg road and the railroad, 300 yards in front of the Nine-miles road.

On his return to these troops, Naglee says: "The enemy had opened a most destructive cross-fire upon them from the pieces near the redoubt that had not been spiked, and this, with the fire from their immediate front, was no longer to be endured, and they were withdrawn and marched down the Nine-miles road, and placed in position in rear of this road, about 300 yards from the Seven Pines, when soon their services were [again] required."

Casey's troops had resisted for two hours and more a very determined attack in front; and fell back, fighting, after their left flank was turned, and an enfilade and reverse fire, within short range, was brought to bear upon the rifle-pits.

The second line of defense, held by Couch's division, was composed of Peck's brigade, five regiments, on the south side of the Williamsburg road; Devens's brigade, three regiments, across that road; and Abercrombie's brigade, five regiments, on the right. Two regiments and a battery of the latter brigade were detached, guarding the depot of supplies at Fair Oaks station. In describing the operations in the second line, General Keyes says: "As the pressure on Casey's division became greater, he applied to me for re-enforcements. I continued to send them as long as I had troops to spare. . . . The Ninety-third Pennsylvania, Peck's brigade, engaged the enemy on the left [of Casey's line] . . . until overwhelming numbers forced him to retire, which he did in good order. . . . I ordered the Fifty-fifth New York . . . to 'save the guns,' meaning some of Casey's. The regiment moved up the Williamsburg road at double-quick, conducted by General Naglee. . . . I ordered Neill's Twenty-third and Rippey's Sixty-first Pennsylvania regiments to move to the support of Casey's right. . . . Under the immediate command of General Couch, these two regiments assailed a vastly superior force of the enemy. . . . Almost immediately after ordering the Twenty-third and Sixty-first to the right, and as soon as they could be reached, I sent the Seventh Massachusetts, Colonel Russell, and the Sixty-second New York, Colonel Riker, to re-enforce them."

But, before either of these four regiments were in position to support Casey's right, the latter's left flank was turned, and the Federal first line of defense was lost. The two regiments ordered to re-enforce Couch in his attempt to relieve the pressure on Casey's right did not reach him, but joined the two reigments that were already at Fair Oaks Station.

General Couch says: "I advanced with Neill's and Rippey's regiments through a close wood, moving by the flank. Directing Neill where to move, and pushing on with Rippey, we at once came upon a large column of the enemy in reserve, but apparently moving towards Fair Oaks. . . . They [Neill and Rippey] immediately engaged, but were finally compelled to retire. . . . Here Colonel Rippey and all his field officers fell, and in twenty minutes the enemy had passed over the [Ninemiles] road leading to my centre, cutting off the advance at Fair Oaks, now re-enforced by the Seventh Massachusetts . . . and Sixty-second New York . . . ordered up by General Keyes."

In speaking of this engagement, General Keyes says: "Both regiments were badly cut up. . . . The casualties of the Sixty-first amount to 263 and are heavier than in any other regiment in Couch's division. After this attack the Twenty-third took part in the hard fighting which closed the day near Seven Pines. The Sixty-first withdrew in detachments, some of which came again into action near my headquarters."

In the meanwhile events of interest were taking place in the immediate vicinity of Seven Pines. General Devens, in his official report says: "At about 4 P. M., the line of General Casey then having been driven back, . . . an order was received from General Keyes that the Tenth Massachusetts should advance up the Richmond [Williamsburg] road through the felled timber and endeavor to hold the ground in front. Colonel Briggs moved accordingly up the road, . . . [and] found himself immediately assailed on the left flank and rear by heavy volleys of musketry. . . . Colonel Briggs gallantly struggled . . . to maintain his position. From the nature of the ground, entirely covered with fallen timber, it was not possible for him to effect this [necessary change of front], and the left wing was soon thrown into much confusion from the heavy fire of the enemy.

... I directed Colonel Briggs to fall back and re-form the regiment at the rifle-pits before occupied by him. ... It was not possible for him to effect this in good order; but at a short distance behind the Fair Oaks [Nine-miles] road Colonel Briggs rallied his regiment successfully and led it forward in good order to the position indicated. Re-enforcements arrived in a short time and were thrown forward to the left and front."

Thus, the Tenth Massachusetts, of Couch's division, after a few minutes' experience in the second abatis, could not, at first, be rallied in their own vacant rifle-pits, in the second line of defense.

Keyes's affairs were then in a very critical condition. A large portion of Casey's troops, in falling back from their earthworks, had been thrown into, almost, inextricable confusion whilst crossing the second abatis under destructive cross-fire, and had left the field; the two regiments under Couch, on the right, had been badly cut up, one of them routed and out of the fight, exposing the right flank and rear of Couch's earthworks; four regiments and a battery were cut off north of Fair Oaks; one of Devens's regiments on the Williamsburg road had been hurled back from the felled timber in disorder; and the Confederates were pressing into the second abatis and in the woods south of the road, seriously threatening the left flank of Couch's main line. Such was the state of things with Keyes when the leading regiment of Berry's brigade, of Kearney's division of Heintzelman's corps, reached Seven Pines.

About noon, May 31, Berry's brigade halted at the third line of defense on the Williamsburg road, having come up that morning from Bottom's Bridge; and Birney's brigade reached that line of defense, but near the railroad, almost at the same time.

General Kearney, in his official report, says: "At 3 P. M. I received an order to send a brigade of my division by the railroad to support Keyes's corps, said to be severely engaged. Birney's brigade was designated, and getting most promptly under arms, advanced accordingly.* Captain Hunt, Aide to General Heint-

---

*Owing to subsequent conflict of orders, for which General Birney was not responsible, his brigade was not in action that day.—G. W. S.

zelman, arriving from the field, made me aware of the discomfiture of most of Casey's division. The retiring wagons and a dense stream of disorganized fugitives arrived nearly simultaneously.
. . . I, however, soon received General Heintzelman's directions to order forward by the Williamsburg road the remaining brigade [Berry's], and to retrieve the position the enemy had driven us from. I put myself at the head of the advanced regiment and set forward without delay. I also sent written orders for Jameson's brigade, camped at the *tete-de-pont*, near Bottom's Bridge (three miles in rear), to come up without delay. This order met with General Heintzelman's approval. On arriving at the field of battle we found certain zig-zag rifle-pits sheltering crowds of men and the enemy firing from abatis and timber in their front.
. . . I had but the Third Michigan up, but they moved forward with alacrity, dashing into the felled timber, and commenced a desperate but determined contest."

General Kearney speaks of the prompt coming up of other regiments of Berry's brigade and their hard fighting and steady advance in the felled timber, and the woods on the south side of the Williamsburg road; re-enforced later by two regiments of Jameson's brigade that arrived from Bottom's Bridge.

General Berry, in his official report, says: "We steadily drove the enemy so far that I had serious fears of being flanked. . . . We were at this time in the woods extending from the edge of the slashings below, up the woods and on the left of the camping ground of General Casey's division, completely commanding his old camp and the earthworks with our rifles."

In the meantime the contest continued across the *abatis* in front of Couch's main line. Whilst Keyes's left flank was protected by Kearney's advance in the woods on the south side of the Williamsburg road, the danger to his right flank became more and more imminent after Naglee's detached regiments had been withdrawn, and Couch's two regiments, farther to the right, had been so badly cut up. The Confederates, on that side, had now crossed the Nine-miles road and were moving toward Seven Pines, on ground east of that road.

General Keyes says: "To make head against the enemy approaching"—from the direction of Fair Oaks—"it was found necessary to effect an almost perpendicular change of front of the troops on the right of the Williamsburg road. . . . This line long resisted the progress of the enemy with the greatest firmness and gallantry, but by pressing it very closely by overwhelming numbers, probably ten[*] to one, they were enabled finally to force it to fall back so far upon the left and centre as to form a new line in rear. . . . Seeing the torrent of enemies continually advancing, I hastened across to the left beyond the fork to bring forward re-enforcements. Brigadier-General Peck" with two regiments, " was ordered, with the concurrence of General Heintzelman, to advance across the open space and attack the enemy, now coming forward in great numbers. . . . After contending against enormous odds those two regiments were forced to give way, Peck, and " one regiment " crossing the Williamsburg road to the wood," the other regiment " passing to the right [along that road], where they took post in the last line of battle, formed mostly after 6 P. M. . . . As soon as Peck had moved forward I hastened to the Tenth Massachusetts, Colonel Briggs, which regiment I had myself once before moved, now in the rifle-pits on the left of the Williamsburg road, and ordered them to follow me across the field. . . . After seeing the Tenth Massachusetts and the adjoining line well at work under a murderous fire, I observed that that portion of the line 150 yards to my left was crumbling away, some falling and others retiring. I perceived also that the artillery had withdrawn, and that large bodies of broken troops were leaving the centre and moving down the Williamsburg road to the rear. . . . I tried in vain to check the retreating current. . . . I found General Heintzelman and other officers engaged in rallying the men, and in a very short time a large number were induced to face about."

Before describing the fighting that occurred, later, on this part of the field, attention is called to those two regiments of Naglee's brigade which had held position to the right of Casey's main line after the latter was driven from the earthworks. General Naglee says that when he " was compelled to retreat about

---

[*] But, see Confederate official reports that will be quoted later.

500 yards" toward Seven Pines, these two regiments formed line with the Sixty-seventh New York, facing the enemy now advancing from the direction of Fair Oaks; and adds: "The men were ordered to lie down, that they should escape the murderous fire that was incessantly pouring in from the front. Scarcely was this done when the Eighty-seventh New York* . . . came along the Nine-miles road with rapid step, cheering most vociferously, passed" the three regiments in Naglee's line "about fifty yards, received a volley, broke, and passed [to the rear], the whole of them running over the backs of those lying down, the latter remaining undisturbed until ordered to rise and meet the accumulating force that was bearing all before it. Volley after volley was given and received. An order was given to charge, but 100 yards brought us into such close proximity with the enemy that a sheet of fire was blazing in our faces. The ranks on both sides were rapidly thinning, but still the great disparity in our number continued. So close were the contending forces, that our men in many instances whilst at a charge poured their fire into the breasts of the enemy within a few feet from the points of their bayonets."

Another portion of Naglee's brigade had "crossed to the left of Couch's position, and advanced 200 yards into and along the woods to the left and in front of the Seven Pines, where they remained actively employed."

It has already been seen that whilst the fighting just described by Generals Keyes and Naglee was going on, Berry's brigade, of Kearney's division, in the woods south of the Williamsburg road, had reached a point "completely commanding" Casey's "old camp and the earthworks." Berry was supported by two regiments of Jameson's brigade; "the other two regiments of that brigade having been diverted—one to Birney and one to Peck." The latter was the Eighty-seventh New York, sent from the left of Couch's line to aid in resisting the advance against Keyes's right flank. The regiment sent to Birney took part only in the last fighting that day on the Williamsburg road.

General Kearney says: It "was perhaps near 6 o'clock when

---

* This regiment was in Jameson's brigade. It did good service on other parts of the field.

our centre and right, defended by troops of the other divisions, with all their willingness, could no longer resist the enemy's right central flank attacks, pushed on with determined discipline and with the impulsion of numerous concentrated masses. Once broken our troops fled incontinently, and a dense body of the enemy pursuing rapidly, yet in order, occupied the Williamsburg road [about three-eighths of a mile east of Seven Pines], the entire open ground, and penetrating deep into the woods," on the south side of that road, "soon interposed between my division and my line of retreat. It was on this occasion that seeing myself cut off, and relying on the high discipline and determined valor of the Thirty-seventh New York Volunteers, I faced them to the rear against the enemy, and held the ground, although so critically placed, and despite the masses that gathered on and had passed us, checked the enemy in his intent of cutting us off against the White Oak Swamp. This enabled the advanced regiments, averted by orders and this contest in their rear, to return from their hitherto victorious career, and to retire by a remaining foot-path known to our scouts (the Saw-mill road), until they once more arrived at and remanned the impregnable position we had left at noon at our own fortified division camp [the Federal third line of defense]." *

Most of Peck's brigade, a portion of Naglee's, and some detached portions of other commands retreated with Kearney's troops. The fighting, however, was continued on the Williamsburg road, east of Seven Pines.

After the Federals, who were retiring on this part of the field, "were induced to face about," as already related by General Keyes, he says : "These were pushed forward and joined to others better organized in the woods, and a line was formed stretching across the [Williamsburg] road in perpendicular direction. General Heintzelman requested me to advance the line on the left of the road, which I did. . . . The last line, formed of portions of Couch's and Casey's divisions and a portion of Kearney's division [one of Jameson's regiments that had been sent to Birney],

---

* It will be seen later that this "grand commotion" was caused by three Confederate regiments only.

checked the advance of the enemy and finally repulsed * him, and this was the beginning of the victory, which on the following day was so gloriously completed."

In Keyes's corps there were eight batteries of artillery; seven of which were actively engaged in the contest around Seven Pines, and one was detached, "cut off," at Fair Oaks. None of the artillery of Heintzelman's corps was brought to the front because of the miry condition of the ground. The Federal official reports give great credit to their artillery in this action.

General Keyes says "the number actually engaged" in his corps "did not amount to more than 12,000;" from which there should be deducted four regiments and one battery, north of Fair Oaks, not engaged in the action on the Williamsburg road. He adds: "The Confederates outnumbered us, during a great part of the conflict, at least four to one, and they were fresh, drilled troops, led on and cheered by their best generals and the President of their Republic. They are right when they assert that the Yankees stubbornly contested every foot of ground. Of nine generals of the Fourth Corps [his own] who were present on the field, all, with one exception, were wounded or his horse was hit in the battle. A large proportion of all the field officers in the action were killed, wounded, or their horses were struck. These facts denote the fierceness of the contest."

The Federal losses in this action numbered 3,351; of which 1,426 were in Casey's † division, 1,042 in Couch's ‡ and 883 in Kearney's. §

About sunset, May 31, one-half of Hooker's division of Heintzelman's corps came up and bivouacked that night on the Williamsburg road a few hundred yards east of the third line of defense; Keyes's corps occupied that part of this line which was south of the road; two brigades of Kearney's division were in the rifle-pits of that line, north of the road, extending nearly

---

* But, see official report of Colonel Jenkins, Confederate, which will be given later.

† Naglee's brigade, 639; Wessells's, 358; Palmer's, 392; artillery, 37.

‡ Abercrombie's brigade, 563; Devens's, 173; Peck's, 298; artillery, 8. Not including the losses in two regiments of Abercrombie's, one of Devens's, one of Peck's; and one battery "cut off" north of Fair Oak Station.

§ Berry's brigade, 464; Jameson's, 419.

to the railroad; and Birney's brigade was in advance, on the railroad. Early next morning the scattered fragments of the eight raw regiments of Casey's division—that had been so badly broken up whilst retiring through the second abatis, under close and deadly fire—were rallied and placed in position at the third line of defense.

The result of the fighting that day, on the Williamsburg road, was to throw back Keyes's corps from the vicinity of Seven Pines, and bring up Heintzelman's corps from Bottom's Bridge and White Oak Bridge; thus uniting these two corps, at night May 31, in a strong position at the third line of defense. One brigade and a half being left in rear to guard the above-named bridges.

Confederate Accounts.—Bearing in mind what was said in the preliminary chapter concerning the movement of troops in the Confederate right wing under Longstreet, it will, perhaps, be no surprise to find—in what will presently be stated—that the Federal commanders greatly overrated the numbers by which they were attacked.

General D. H. Hill, in his official report, says: "At 1 o'clock the signal guns were fired, and my division moved off in fine style." "Rodes's brigade on the right of the [Williamsburg] road, supported by Rains's brigade; Garland on the left, supported by G. B. Anderson. Each wing was preceded by a regiment deployed as skirmishers. Having been long delayed in waiting for the relieving force the right wing did not advance for a quarter of an hour after the left. This exposed Garland and Anderson to the whole Yankee force. The right wing was hurried forward and came up handsomely, preserving the line, although wading through the mud and water in places two or three feet deep."

Brigadier-General Samuel Garland, Jr., in his official report, says: "Upon hearing the signal the line of skirmishers promptly advanced into the woods in front, and the brigade followed, moving by the right flanks of regiments at deploying distance. . . . Col. George B. Anderson, commanding [a brigade] moved a quarter of a mile in rear as a support. . . . My line of skirmishers had advanced only a few hundred yards when they encountered that of the enemy. The difficulties of the ground were almost insurmountable. The recent rains had formed ponds of water throughout the woods, with mud at the bottom, through which the men waded knee-deep, and occasionally sinking to the hips in boggy places, almost beyond the hope of extrication. The forest was so thick and the undergrowth so tangled that it was impracticable to see the heads of the several regiments as they moved forward, and the deploying intervals were in consequence very imperfectly preserved. . . . When the skirmishers became heavily engaged the regiments pressed upon their heels and the fire became hot along our whole front before emerging from the woods. The regiments were brought into line of battle to support the skirmishers."

Garland's whole brigade thus struck the small regiment of raw troops sent forward by General Casey to support the Federal picket line. General Garland adds: "We drove the enemy before us out of the woods back into the abatis, where they had several regiments drawn up. . . . We had now reached the edge of the wood, where the abatis impeded our further advance, and the troops were under heavy fire. . . . Hurrying forward in person to the abatis, I found that as the regiments emerged from the woods they overlapped each other as they deployed, and being thus in many places huddled together, were suffering terribly from the enemy's fire. The regimental commanders, who had received my orders to move by the left flank, were unable to effect the movement in good order under the galling fire. The alternative was adopted—to push the regiments forward through the abatis. . . . Meanwhile my regiments had advanced more or less into the abatis, the Second Florida and Thirty-eighth Virginia up to the fence, and driving away the gunners and killing the horses from a section of artillery near the road. We were losing heavily, especially in field and company officers. . . . The entire brigade of five regiments and a battalion was in the front of the fight . . . with only six field officers [not already disabled]. . . . The supporting brigade advancing at this opportune moment, and the passage of lines being a feat in tactics which had never been practiced by any of us, large fragments of those regiments who were left without field or company officers were joined in and continued forward with that brigade." In the meantime General D. H. Hill had ordered Bondurant's battery into action.

Leaving Garland's brigade, re-enforced at a critical moment, in the first abatis, north of the Williamsburg road, by General (then Colonel) G. B. Anderson; attention is called to Rodes's brigade on the south side of that road. In his official report, Brigadier-General R. E. Rodes describes the movement of his brigade through woods similar in character to that encountered by Garland's brigade. Rodes's skirmish line, the Sixth Alabama, under General (then Colonel) John B. Gordon, easily drove back the Federal pickets, the regiment ordered to support these pickets having been already routed by Garland's brigade. Gordon's regiment of skirmishers reached the edge of the woods in good order, and at once entered the abatis in front of the redoubt. The regiments coming up were deployed; the skirmishers were concentrated; the whole brigade was formed in line, and the contest on this part of the field became very hot across the first abatis.

Carter's battery was brought up. General Rodes adds: "I determined to attack from the position I then held, and requested General Rains, who commanded the supporting brigade, through an officer of my staff, and soon after in person, to move forward his brigade through the woods so as to protect my right flank while I attacked the enemy in front; his brigade had a few moments before occupied a line extending from my right obliquely to the front, and at the moment of our conversation was being thrown back on a line parallel to and a little in rear of that occupied by mine. He stated to me that he apprehended an attack on his own right flank, and declined, therefore, to move."

Attention will now be again called to G. B. Anderson's brigade. In his official report he says: "The brigade was put in motion as ordered, by the left flank of regiments, between 1 and 1.30 P. M., so as to be about one-quarter of a mile in rear of Garland's brigade. After moving a short distance, not more than half a mile, word was sent to me from General Garland that he was in great need of re-enforcements. . . . The Fourth North Carolina being on the right and somewhat in advance, came first into action, emerging from the woods half a mile or more in front of the enemy's redoubt and breastworks, upon ground which, up to within 200 or 300 yards of the redoubt, was obstructed by the felling of trees. The other regiments . . . . came up successively. . . . Having started the three regiments on the right fairly into action, I found myself in the woods on the left of the clearing with the Twenty-seventh Georgia, and from the force of circumstances, as the day advanced, remained on this flank during most of the action. This regiment, having formed line in the woods, engaged the enemy there [one regiment of Naglee's brigade detached in support of the Federal picket line south of the railroad] and charged him over a very difficult piece of obstructed ground; but finding itself in the face of a very greatly superior force [two regiments of Naglee's] and in too advanced a position, one, in fact, which endangered its being completely flanked; it was withdrawn a short distance, its left flank thrown back [still fighting] and I went into the clearing to endeavor to procure re-enforcements before again advancing."

In the meanwhile the contest had raged in front of Garland's brigade and three of G. B. Anderson's regiments, just north of the Williamsburg road; and in front of Rodes's brigade, south of that road. General D. H. Hill says, "I now detached General Rains to make a wide flank movement to take the Yankee works in reverse, while Rodes moved steadily to the front. . . . General Rains had now gained the rear of the Yankee redoubt and opened fire on the infantry posted in the woods. I now noticed commotion in the camps and redoubt and indications of evacuating the position. Rodes took skillful advantage of this commotion, and moved up his brigade in beautiful order and took possession of the redoubt and rifle-pits. So rapid was the advance that six pieces were abandoned by the Yankees. These Rodes had turned upon the retreating column with effect. Carter galloped up with his pieces, and these, with the captured guns, successfully repulsed an attempt of fresh Yankee troops to recapture the works."

Brigadier-General Gabriel J. Rains, in his official report, says: "Pursuant to the instructions of Major-General [D. H.] Hill, we penetrated the woods to take the enemy in rear and drive him from his batteries. . . . We found ourselves in a swamp, but pressed on with alacrity until we had gained the rear of the enemy. Here we halted, directed by kind Providence, exactly at the right place, where I made a change of front by a wheel in the thicket, and advancing found ourselves facing the foe. . . . As soon as we reached the edge of the thicket, seeing the enemy in front, I ordered the fire; . . . followed by a long, loud and continued roll of musketry for full fifteen minutes without cessation. I had heard many a volley before, but never one so prolonged and continuous. We evidently were unexpected there, were near at hand to the foe and struck them like an avalanche. Their shot and cannon balls came like hail into the bushes around us, but the men lay close to the ground and only rose up on the knee to fire. The enemy were in great force before us, at least ten to one,* and increasing by re-enforcements, and at their fire about 100 of our men broke to the rear, but happening to be just there I easily rallied them, and they fought like heroes, and more than redeemed the act of a momentary panic. All acquitted themselves well, and when we emerged from the woods and swept through the desolated camp of the enemy, and their dead and wounded, their property lying everywhere around, not one article was taken by the men, who retained their ranks like true soldiers, and ultimately passed the night in line of battle without fire or light in another part of the woods, ready to receive and check the enemy should he advance, also taking a number of prisoners. My brigade was again called upon the next day to resist the enemy, actively engaged out of view with another part of our army, but I presume he had had enough of the fight and carnage for once and did not appear. Our loss in the battle was more than one-seventh of the whole brigade, and of these very few not killed or wounded."

General D. H. Hill, says: "My division had beaten Casey's

---

* But, see the Federal official reports previously quoted.

division and all the re-enforcements brought him, and had driven him and his supports into the woods and swamps. It was desirable, however, to press the Yankees as closely as possible. I therefore sent back to General Longstreet and asked for another brigade. In a few minutes the magnificent brigade of R. H. Anderson came to my support. A portion of this force, under Colonel Jenkins, consisting of the Palmetto Sharpshooters and the Sixth South Carolina, was sent on the extreme left to scour along the railroad and Nine-miles road, and thus get in rear of the enemy, while a portion, under General [R. H.] Anderson, in person, was sent on the immediate left of the redoubt, into the woods, where the Yankees had hid after being repulsed by the fire of Carter's battery and the captured guns."

The Federal force against which R. H. Anderson, in person, was sent, with two regiments, consisted of that portion of Naglee's brigade which had pressed back the Twenty-seventh Georgia, under General G. B. Anderson, a short time before Casey's earthworks were carried. Before following the important movements of R. H. Anderson's brigade on D. H. Hill's left, some account will be given of what occurred, just after that time, on the Confederate right.

General D. H. Hill says: "Dearing's battery had been sent up by General Longstreet, and rendered important service. . . . I now resolved to drive the Yankees out of the woods on the right of the road, where they were still in strong force. [This force was Berry's brigade of Kearney's division, just arrived from the Federal third line of defense.] General Rains was near them, and a written order was carried him by my Adjutant to move farther to the right. I regret that that gallant and meritorious officer did not advance farther in that direction. He would have taken the Yankees in flank, and the direct attack of Rodes in front would have been less bloody. The magnificent brigade of Rodes moved over the open ground to assault the Yankees strongly posted in the woods [south of the Williamsburg road]. He met a most galling fire, and his advance was checked. A portion of his command met with a disastrous repulse. Kemper's brigade was now sent me by General Longstreet, and directed by me to move directly to the support of Rodes. This brigade, however, did not engage the Yankees, and Rodes's men were badly cut up."

General Rodes, in his official report, says: " The Sixth Alabama upon moving across the field in the edge of which they had first halted and entering the woods on the opposite side, driving the enemy before them, encountered a heavy fire of musketry upon its right and front and finally upon the rear of its right wing. Under these circumstances, and finding that my right was not supported by the brigade of General Rains, which was but a short distance behind, . . . I ordered this regiment [Sixth Alabama] to fall back to the position it had last occupied on the edge of the field, where it was about in line with the enemy's intrenchments. . . . I feel decidedly confident that if we had been properly supported in the last charge, the brigade would have marched on with uninterrupted progress. . . . When the Sixth Alabama moved back, the right wing of the Twelfth Alabama . . . retired with it and took position on its left behind the intrenchments [Casey's rifle-pits]. . . . At this time a portion of the Heavy Artillery Battalion [serving as infantry] retired and, I regret to say, headed by their officers, took refuge in the ditches in front of the enemy's redoubt, a position from which I had much difficulty in dislodging them, when they were called upon to man the redoubt. . . . It was evident that nothing could be effected toward an advance while the right wing of the brigade was so exposed. . . . The Fifth Alabama and Twelfth Mississippi [Rodes's left wing] continued to hold their ground steadily [in the second abatis] though subjected to a constant fire from the enemy's musketry, which inflicted a severe loss upon them. Just after the Twelfth Alabama had fallen back and about an hour after the brigade had assumed its most advanced position . . . re-enforcements commenced to arrive and in assisting General Kemper to place his brigade, so that it could move forward to relieve my advanced regiments, . . . I received a wound in the arm, which in a short time became so painful as to compel me to turn over the command of the brigade to Colonel Gordon, of the Sixth Alabama. I did not leave the field, though, until sunset. . . . The total number of men carried into action was about 2,200. The aggregate number present at camp was, however, 2,587."

The official records show the losses in this brigade were in killed and wounded, 1,094; and 5 missing. The Sixth Alabama suffered more severely than any other regiment. It lost 348 killed and wounded, "near sixty per cent. of its aggregate force."

General John B. Gordon, then Colonel, in speaking of the fighting that occurred just before he was ordered to withdraw his regiment, says: "Entering the swamp, covered in water two or three feet deep, in which the vines, briars, and felled timber made an almost impassable barrier, we were driving the enemy steadily before us, when he suddenly moved upon my right flank a strong force [Berry's brigade] bearing Confederate battle-flags and enfiladed my whole line. My adjutant was ordered immediately off to ask for support, but was shot down. Messenger after messenger was then dispatched to urge the troops [Rains's brigade] in rear of my right to move down to my support. This brigade, although within sight and but a few hundred yards distant, failed to give me any assistance whatever. . . . To protect my right and rear it now became necessary to change the front of my right company. . . . In a sheet of fire and within a few rods of overwhelming numbers this company stood until the last officer and non-commissioned officer—except one corporal—and forty-four of the fifty-six men carried into action—had fallen. Yet, when General Rodes gave the order for this regiment to fall back, the few survivors were loading and firing, all undaunted, amid their fallen comrades. . . . Contending from the first with superior numbers, flanked on the right and unsupported by reserves, officers and men falling thick and fast, if not killed possibly to drown in the water in which they stood, there was no sign of wavering in any portion of the line. Two field officers had fallen, three companies had not an officer spared, four others had but one [each], and more than half of these brave men had fallen, when, under orders, they retired to the enemy's intrenchments in the rear."

In the records I find nothing that tends to explain or to justify the inaction of Rains's brigade after Casey's camp was captured.

It is not necessary to dwell upon the effect that would probably have followed had this brigade made a determined movement against Berry's left flank and rear, when far advanced in the woods, south of the Williamsburg road, "on the left of the camping ground of General Casey's division."

In his official report of the operations of Rodes's brigade, after he was placed in command of it, General Gordon says: "Although Brigadier General Rodes did not retire from the field in one hour and a half after he was wounded, and not until the firing had entirely ceased [on that part of the field], he was compelled from exhaustion to turn over the command of the brigade. Notified that I was placed in command, I reported to Major-General [D. H.] Hill for orders. Under his direction I moved the brigade about half a mile to the rear, and ordered them to encamp on either side of the Williamsburg road, spending nearly the entire night with large details from the brigade in nursing the wounded whom the surgeons had been unable to remove."

On Rodes's left Garland's brigade, and three regiments of G. B. Anderson's brigade—more or less intermingled—had been engaged in front of, and in, the second abatis. General Garland says: "Late in the afternoon I succeeded in separating and reorganizing my command, and held it under orders in reserve. Sleeping upon the field of battle, this brigade, along with Colonel Anderson's, was held in reserve on Sunday, the 1st instant." He states that the strength of his brigade was 2,065, and that the killed and wounded numbered 698; missing, 42.

General G. B. Anderson says that the three regiments of his brigade that supported Garland, "being exhausted and cut up and to some extent scattered, and the ground being held by fresher troops, I proceeded, as the evening closed in, to collect them together at a point in the rear portion of the clearing to the left of the road. After night we were ordered by the Major-General commanding the division to take position in the woods in rear of the clearing, where we spent the night." He states the brigade went into action 1,865 strong, and lost in killed and wounded 829; missing, 37. The heaviest losses were in the

Fourth North Carolina. Out of 678 carried into action, this regiment lost 353 killed and wounded; missing, 6.

It is thus seen that three brigades of D. H. Hill's division, after five or six hours of bloody fighting, were withdrawn from the second abatis, and bivouacked that night in the edge of the woods west of the first abatis. Re-enforcements had at last come up in full force. It has already been shown, by General Rains's report, that his brigade "ultimately passed the night in line of battle, without fire or light, in another part of the woods, ready to receive and check the enemy should he advance"!

Attention will now be called to the arrival of re-enforcements in such numbers that D. H. Hill was enabled to withdraw his brigades from the front line. These re-enforcements were the five brigades—three of Longstreet's, followed by two of Huger's—from the Charles City road to the Williamsburg road. It has already been stated, the head of that column of five brigades reached the latter road, far in rear of the fighting, at 5 P.M.

In his official report General Wilcox says: "The leading regiment . . . was ordered immediately to the front by the division commander [Longstreet] to report to Major-General D. H. Hill. . . . Soon after . . . [another regiment] received similar orders. I was directed to place Colston's brigade in rear of the right flank of the troops then engaged; this being accomplished, I moved forward in command of the two remaining regiments of my own brigade . . . and reported to General D. H. Hill. The [first regiment that had been sent forward] . . . had been ordered by General Hill to report to General Kemper; the latter ordered three companies of this regiment to dislodge the enemy holding a certain point that proved to be very annoying to our line. Colonel Moore took command of these companies, dislodging the enemy, receiving two wounds, one of which proved mortal, his horse being killed at the same time. This affair occasioned a loss of 66 killed and wounded in a few minutes."

It will be borne in mind that General D. H. Hill, in his official report, says: "Kemper's brigade" was "directed by me to move directly to the support of Rodes. This brigade, however, did not engage the Yankees, and Rodes's men were badly cut up." But it seems that, later, this brigade being "annoyed" by musketry fire from the woods south of the Williamsburg road, Kemper ordered three companies of the leading regiment of Wilcox's brigade, just brought forward from the Charles City road, to "dislodge the enemy." That enemy was the Federal rear guard, stationed there by General Kearney to cover the withdrawal of his troops. The manner in which the "three companies" did the work assigned them by General Kemper is sufficient evidence of what the "five brigades" from the Charles City road would have done if they had been promptly put in close action by General Longstreet, to support the attack made by D. H. Hill, at 1 P. M.

General Wilcox adds: "On reporting to General Hill he directed me to form in line with three of my regiments in the edge of the woods beyond [south of] the field in which were the captured batteries and rifle-pits of the enemy [Casey's line]. A feeble fire from the enemy continued in the woods for some ten or fifteen minutes after my line was formed, and then ceased. The fire, however, on the left of the road continued until after dark, and at times with great vivacity, and on this side the enemy had been driven much farther."

The fire referred to by General Wilcox, which "continued until after dark," was on the Williamsburg road, a short distance east of Seven Pines, where Heintzelman and Keyes made their last attempt that day to drive back the advancing Confederates. The other brigades from the Charles City road followed after Wilcox's brigade, and went into bivouac on and near the open ground around Casey's captured earthworks. At that time Mahone's brigade was in observation well out on the Charles City road, and Pickett's brigade was far back on the railroad. It remains to account for but one of the thirteen brigades which composed the right wing under Longstreet—" the magnificent brigade of R. H. Anderson," sent to the front, at D. H. Hill's request, by General Longstreet, after Hill's division, unaided, "had beaten Casey's division and all the re-enforcements brought him."

It will be recalled that two regiments of this brigade, under General R. H. Anderson, in person, were sent into the woods north of the redoubt, where two regiments of Naglee's brigade still held position. No official Confederate report of the details of this operation seems to have been made. But there is no doubt of the correctness of General Naglee's statement that: "The enemy had opened a most destructive cross-fire upon them [his two regiments] from the pieces near the redoubt that had not been spiked, and this, with the fire [of the two regiments under R. H. Anderson] from their immediate front was no longer to be endured, and they [Naglee's two regiments] were withdrawn."

Reference will now be made to the operations of two regiments of R. H. Anderson's brigade under Colonel Jenkins, ordered by D. H. Hill to move to "the extreme left to scour along the railroad [far in advance of Pickett's brigade] and [along] the Nine-miles road, and thus get in rear of the enemy." It will be remembered that on the part of the field to which these two regiments were ordered, the Twenty-seventh Georgia, under General G. B. Anderson, in person, had been engaged with varying success, whilst the rest of D. H. Hill's division was attacking Casey's line; and that G. B. Anderson "went into the clearing to endeavor to procure re-enforcements before again advancing." The latter says: "Colonel Jenkins's regiment . . . and the Sixth South Carolina Volunteers were sent with me, and as soon as they could be formed in line . . . the three regiments again charged in the best style over the same piece of obstructed ground [on which the Twenty-seventh Georgia had previously fought], . . . through the woods beyond, . . . routing him completely."

This was the affair described by General Couch in which Rippey's regiment and Neill's regiment were so quickly, and so "badly cut up." General G. B. Anderson adds: "The Georgia regiment, having been in action much longer than the South Carolina, and being somewhat scattered and very much fatigued, was now halted and reformed in line. The South Carolina regiments advanced some distance farther, and after a short time became [again] engaged with the enemy. I sent to General R. H. Anderson, who I learned was then in advance, and informed him of the position of the [Twenty-seventh Georgia] Regiment. He came himself and conducted it with me to a position where it was placed in line of battle. I then left it and went to look after the rest of the brigade." The disposition he made of the latter, for the night, under instructions of General D. H. Hill, has already been stated.

It appears from the records that, whilst General Wilcox commanded the three brigades of Longstreet's division that were on the Nine-miles road, three and one-half miles from Richmond, May 30, General R. H. Anderson commanded the three brigades of that division which were in camp north of Richmond, and Colonel M. Jenkins, of the Palmetto regiment, was temporarily in command of R. H. Anderson's brigade. When that brigade was ordered to the front, General R. H. Anderson accompanied it, but did not relieve Colonel Jenkins of its executive command. When General D. H. Hill detached two regiments to go with General G. B. Anderson, Colonel Jenkins accompanied those regiments, and General R. H. Anderson took control of the rest of the brigade in the attack against General Naglee's two regiments, as already stated.

In his official report, Colonel Jenkins speaks of the "Twenty-eighth Georgia" when he means the "Twenty-seventh." In the following quotations the latter is substituted for the former.

Colonel Jenkins says: "Guided by Col. George B. Anderson to the left of the Twenty-seventh Georgia (one of his regiments), [I] took position against a small abatis with my left company deployed near the York River Railroad and my right adjacent to the Twenty-seventh Georgia. Col. John Bratton, with the Sixth South Carolina Volunteers, having afterwards come up, took position on the right of the Twenty-seventh Georgia, and an advance being concerted, the regiments moved forward across the abatis under fire. Not being able, on account of the thick undergrowth, to see the enemy, I moved my regiment forward without firing and with fixed bayonets."

Colonel Jenkins describes the affair in which Neill's and Rippey's regiments were so badly "cut up," and adds: "Our advance was now continued, with little or no opposition, . . . across a neighborhood road leading to [the] railroad. Here the lines were halted and dressed . . . and at this time, seeing General Richard H. Anderson, I reported to him. His instructions being to advance, we went forward to the second abatis, a very heavy and difficult one to pass. At this point, the railroad being open to view and some of the enemy being seen to our left and front, I threw out skirmishers to feel it. . . . I [then] advanced my regiment through the abatis under a very heavy fire. . . . Finding after crossing that the Sixth regiment . . . and mine were isolated, I instructed Colonel Bratton to keep his left touching to my right and the enemy's line, after a stubborn resistance, having given way to our attack, . . . I executed under fire from the right front a change of front obliquely forward on right company. Directing the two regiments forward in line, we drove the enemy to the front and right. . . . At this point the enemy, heavily re-enforced, made a desperate stand, and our fighting was within seventy-five yards. Not pausing even to load, and pouring in my volleys at close range as I advanced, I never allowed a broken line to get through their new lines before I pushed on the new line and drove them back, losing heavily myself, but killing numbers of the enemy. Our advance continued in this steady manner, the enemy steadily giving back. The ranks of the enemy having broken to our right and front and the fire having lessened, I halted the lines, dressed them, and then changed front obliquely forward."

Having crossed the Nine-miles road at a point only a few hundred yards south of the railroad, the first change of front, obliquely to the right, caused the general movement of Jenkins's line, on the east of the Nine-miles road, to be towards the southeast; his second change of front made the direction of his advance nearly south, almost at right angles to the Williamsburg road, on a line crossing the latter at a point about three-eighths of a mile east of Seven Pines.

Continuing his report, he says : " Following the retreating enemy either fresh troops or heavy re-enforcements met us, and . . . offered us battle with greatly superior numbers. Without pausing our lines moved on him, and our steady advance was not to be resisted. After a most obstinate resistance and terrible slaughter the enemy gave back to our left and right across the Williamsburg road, about a mile or more from General Casey's headquarters. [A portion of these beaten Federals fell back on the Williamsburg road and the other portion fell back south of that road]. Following the latter and heavier body, they were again re-enforced and took position in a wood parallel [to] and about 300 yards on the right [south] of the Williamsburg road. With the Sixth Regiment . . . and six companies of my regiment in line on the Williamsburg road, and with five companies sweeping the remnant of the enemy who had retired to our left, I was fired upon by our battery near General Casey's headquarters, the fire enfilading my line in the road and leading me to believe that I had gotten too far in the enemy's rear, but on sending notice of my position to General [D. H.] Hill the fire was stopped. . . . At this moment Major William Anderson, then commanding my regiment, reported to me a heavy column of the enemy advancing on me by the Williamsburg road, and being then engaged with superior numbers in my front and not wishing to retire, I determined to break the enemy in front before I could be reached by this new advance, and then by a change of front to meet them. I sent . . . to get re-enforcements either from General [R. H.] Anderson or General [D. H.] Hill, and ordering Major William Anderson to fight the advance of the column on the Williamsburg road, . . . I carried forward swiftly and steadily my line against the enemy [south of that road]. Having to pass across an open field on this advance, I lost heavily, but succeeded in routing and dispersing the enemy in my front driving them at least a quarter of a mile. . . . In the meanwhile, Major William Anderson, advancing down the Williamsburg road and firing upon the enemy's advanced skirmishers, they retired to the advancing column, and in the momentary check gave me time to make my dispositions to meet them. Having dressed the lines, I moved by the flank . . . and took up line of battle oblique to the [Williamsburg] road; . . . so as to present front at once to the enemy's advance by the road and to any rallied party that might recover from my last attack. . . . [It was then] reported to me the Twenty-seventh Georgia [was] about 300 yards to my rear, and I sent . . . to bring them up at the double-quick. During this time we had evidence of the near approach of the enemy by hearing their words of command and their cheers. . . . The enemy [was now reported] in line of battle, advancing at the double-quick. Strengthened by the nearness of support, I advanced my line toward them also at the double-quick, and assumed a position perpendicular to the Williamsburg road in the open field along the crest of a hill, the woods immediately in front, and the enemy in line about one hundred yards distant. The Twenty-seventh Georgia was placed on the right, touching to the road; my regiment . . . in centre, and the Sixth Regiment on left. The enemy poured in a heavy fire; . . . the supporting regiment, under a terrible fire, gave back. . . . The enemy, encouraged, redoubled his fire; . . . cheered and advanced, and I determined to meet him. In prompt obedience the two regiments rose from their knees, from whence they had been firing upon the enemy with decided effect, and resumed their old, steady advance, firing full in face of the foe. The two lines neared each other to thirty or forty yards, and now the left of my regiment and the Sixth South Carolina Volunteers passing the swamp, came full upon the enemy's right. Losing heavily, I pressed on, and the enemy sullenly and slowly gave way. . . . Driving them in this way, we had advanced some 200 or 300 yards, the enemy getting more and more disordered and beginning to break badly. By this time . . . the Fifth South Carolina . . . came up at the double quick. The Twenty-seventh Georgia . . . rallied and came forward on my right. . . . [The Fifth South Carolina] . . . came up on their right, sweeping . . . the rallied fragments who had collected and resumed fire from the woods to the right, and thus, at 7.40 P.M., we closed our busy day. . . . Night having settled upon the field, I posted in this extreme position, with instructions to throw out pickets, the Nineteenth Mississippi Regiment [of Wilcox's brigade], which . . . had now arrived. I retired the other regiments to the enemy's camp in rear [at Seven Pines] where we reposed for the night, my regiment sleeping in the camp of the Tenth Massachusetts Volunteers [of Devens's brigade]. . . . We passed in our march through two abatis of fallen timber, over four camps, and artillery twice, driving the enemy from three pieces. . . .

The service we did will be evidenced by our list of killed and wounded. . . . Out of 11 in the color guard, 10 were shot down. . . . Captain Carpenter . . . advanced by my colors until his gallant little band of 28 dwindled to 12 ; . . . when the fatal ball pierced his heart."

The official records do not show the number of casualties in either of the two South Carolina regiments that were sent by D. H. Hill to "the extreme left to scour along the railroad and Nine-miles road." But, Colonel John Bratton, commanding the Sixth South Carolina, says the losses in his regiment that day were 269 in killed and wounded, out of 521 taken into action. It is probable that the losses in the Palmetto Sharpshooters were in number about the same. General George B. Anderson's official report shows that the losses in the Twenty-seventh Georgia, which supported these two South Carolina regiments, were 145, in killed and wounded, out of 392 carried into action.

It is believed that the annals of war show few, if any, instances of more persistent, skillful and effective "battle-field fighting" than was done by the two South Carolina regiments, under Colonel Jenkins, in the afternoon of May 31.

In the meanwhile, Pickett's brigade, under Longstreet's order, was held back on the railroad "to repel any advance of the enemy up that road"! Of the five brigades from the Charles City road, only three companies were put in close action. The Confederate successes were gained by the four brigades of D. H. Hill's division aided, after 4 P. M., by but one of the six brigades of Longstreet's division. Yet, General Longstreet attributes "the failure of complete success," that day, "to the slow movements of General Huger's command," and claims that the hardest part of the battle was thrown on his "own poor division"!!

The losses in three brigades of D. H. Hill's division are officially reported to have been 2,705, of which 740 were in Garland's brigade; 866 in G. B. Anderson's; and 1,099 in Rodes's. The losses in Rains's brigade are officially reported "more than one-seventh of the whole brigade." It may be safely stated that the losses in D. H. Hill's division were about 3,000.

CHAPTER III.

Alleged "Slow Movements" of Huger's Division.

GENERAL LONGSTREET says : " Our plan was " " to turn your [the Federal] left by moving Huger's command across the head of White Oak Swamp ; that to be followed by the attack of General D. H. Hill . . ."*

Previous to the recent publication of the "Official Records" the weight of evidence, so far as it was generally made known, seemed to give color of probability to the above statement; which constitutes the foundation upon which is based the censure cast upon Huger by Generals Longstreet and Johnston. Investigation, however, at a later period, developed the fact that Longstreet, himself, was directly responsible for the movements of Huger's division. This fact would exonerate Huger, even if he had been ordered by General Johnston "to make a strong flank movement around the left of the enemy's position and attack him in rear of that flank."

But, General Johnston's written instructions to Huger have now been published, and it is very clearly seen that General Longstreet has misstated their import. In view of those instructions, it is plain that the very severe censure to which Huger has been, to this day, widely subjected, is not founded upon facts. To facilitate a fair comprehension of the whole question an outline of the various phases of the controversy will be given.

The first intimation that the failure of the Confederates to achieve complete success was due to the slow movements of General Huger's command, is found in a letter dated June 7, 1862, written by General Longstreet to General Johnston. At that time General Johnston was disabled by very severe wounds. General Longstreet commanded the right wing of Johnston's army in the

---

* See *Century Magazine*, May, 1885, p. 127.

battle. That wing was composed of three divisions—Longstreet's, D. H. Hill's and Huger's.

The following is a copy of the letter above referred to:

"HEADQUARTERS,
June 7, 1862, 11 A. M.

"*General Johnston, C. S. A.:*

"GENERAL—Your kind favor and present are received. I hope you won't think that I could visit the city without doing myself the pleasure to see you the first thing. I have desired to go in every day, and for no other purpose, but I have been afraid to leave my command for a single moment. It has so turned out that I might have done so, but I did not know it. Not knowing what moment I may be called upon, I am afraid to move. I shall not fail you the first moment that I consider safe.

"The failure of complete success on Saturday [May 31], I attribute to the slow movements of General Huger's command. This threw, perhaps, the hardest part of the battle upon my own poor division. It is greatly cut up, but as true and ready as ever. Our ammunition was nearly exhausted when Whiting moved, and I could not therefore move on with the rush that we could had his movement been earlier. We did advance, however, through three encampments and only stopped at nightfall. The enemy ran in great confusion, but the troops were arranged *en echelon*, and we encountered fresh troops every few hundred yards. These readily fell back, however, as the fleeing ones came to them closely pursued.

"I can't but help think that a display of his forces on the left flank of the enemy by General Huger would have completed the affair and given Whiting as easy and pretty a game as was ever had upon a battle field. Slow men are a little out of place upon the field. Altogether it was very well, but I can't help but regret that it was not complete.

"With kindest expressions for Mrs. Johnston and the members of your staff,

"I remain, truly and sincerely yours,

"JAMES LONGSTREET."[*]

---

[*] "Official Records," Vol XI., Part III., p. 580.

The facts, stated and proved in the preceding chapters, in regard to the bloody and persistent fighting, May 31, by D. H. Hill's division and one brigade of Longstreet's division, are not in accord with that portion of the above letter in which General Longstreet says: "The enemy ran in great confusion;" "we encountered fresh troops every few hundred yards. These readily fell back, however, as the fleeing ones came to them closely pursued."

In presenting to General Johnston the above "rose-colored view" of the successes obtained by the five Confederate brigades that did the fighting on the Williamsburg road, May 31, it is more than probable General Longstreet was endeavoring to show that there was no occasion for him to put more than one of the six brigades of his own division in close action that day. But it is hard to account for his claim that the "slow movements of General Huger's command" threw "the hardest part of the battle on" Longstreet's "own poor division."

Soon after the letter of June 7, 1862, appeared in the published "Official Records," I wrote to General D. H. Hill asking him what he thought of the claim that "the hardest part of the battle," May 31, was thrown upon Longstreet's division? In reply, dated May 22, 1885, General Hill said: "I have been looking over the Rebellion Record and cannot find that letter of Longstreet to Johnston, of June 7, in which he speaks of the suffering of his 'poor division.' Longstreet was not on the field at all on the 31st of May, and did not see any of the fighting." "But he ought to have known that I got no assistance from him except the brigade of R. H. Anderson." "I was much hurt by Longstreet's claim, at the time, of the victory as his. I was still more hurt that the ten pieces captured by my men were turned over to Longstreet's division."

On the 13th of June, 1885, Hill wrote: "The Longstreet letter to Joe Johnston is a reality. I am sorry, sorry, sorry that it is so. But it relieves my mind in regard to General Johnston. I always felt that he had done my division great injustice in his report; but with such a letter from the supposed commander on the field, how could he report differently?"

January 13, 1886, Hill added: "I have not felt kindly to

Longstreet since I read that letter of his to Joe Johnston in the Record of the Rebellion. I can't understand how he had the brass to write such a letter."

General Longstreet's official report is dated June 10, 1862. In that report he said: "The division of General Huger was intended to make a strong flank movement around the left of the enemy's position and attack him in rear of that flank."

General Johnston, in his official report, dated June 24, 1862, said: "General Huger with his division was to move down the Charles City road in order to attack in flank the troops who might be engaged with Hill and Longstreet."

Fortunately for General Huger's reputation, the written instructions given to him by General Johnston are found in the recently published "Official Records."

On May 30, 1862, 8.40 P. M., General Johnson wrote to General Huger. "The reports of Major-General D. H. Hill give me the impression that the enemy is in considerable strength in his front. It seems to me necessary that we should increase our force also. For that object I wish to concentrate the troops of your division on the Charles City road and concentrate the troops of Major-General Hill on that to Williamsburg. To do this it will be necessary for you to move as early in the morning as possible to relieve the brigade of General Hill's division now on the Charles City road. I have desired General Hill to send you a guide. The road is the second large one diverging to the right from the Williamsburg road; the first turns off near the toll-gate. On reaching your position on the Charles City road learn at once the routes to the main roads to Richmond on your right and left, especially to the left, and try to find guides. Be ready, if an action should be begun on your left, to fall upon the enemy's left flank." "P. S.—It is important to move very early." *

On May 31—hour not stated—General Johnston wrote to Huger: "I fear that in my note of last evening, of which there is no copy, I was too positive on the subject of your attacking the enemy's left flank. It will, of course, be necessary for you to

---

* "Official Records," Vol. XI., Part I., p. 938.

know what force is before you first. I hope to be able to have that ascertained for you by cavalry. As our main force will be on your left, it will be necessary for your progress to the front to conform at first to that of General Hill. If you find no strong body in your front, it will be well to aid General Hill; but then a strong reserve should be retained to cover our right." *

Whilst there can be no doubt that General Johnston, on the 30th, intended to concentrate the larger portion of his army against the Federals in the vicinity of Seven Pines—attack them early on the morning of the 31st—and, if possible, overwhelm them before they could be re-enforced; it is very clear that the foregoing written instructions did not require Huger's division to initiate that attack. On the contrary, there is, in documents previously referred to, positive evidence that "the combined movement which had been planned" required that Longstreet's division—moving on the Nine-miles road—should be promptly put in action on D. H. Hill's left, and closely support the attack Hill's division was to make against the Federals on the Williamsburg road. Longstreet misunderstood the direction in which his division was to move into action—General Johnston determined not to make Longstreet's "misunderstanding" generally known—the latter misrepresented the orders Huger received—endeavored to make it appear that the failure of the Confederates to achieve complete success was due to the inexcusable "slow movements of General Huger's command"—and General Johnston sided with General Longstreet.

General Johnston's instructions show that Huger's first and main duty was to guard against the approach of the Federals, on the Charles City road, from the vicinity of White Oak Bridge—where it was known there had been, for several days, a large force of infantry, artillery and cavalry. There is not enough of the "spirit of fight" in the orders given to Huger, by General Johnston, to justify the latter in asserting that "Huger with his division was to move down the Charles City road in order to attack in flank the troops who might be engaged with Hill and Longstreet."

---

* "Official Records," Vol. XI., Part I., p. 938.

ALLEGED SLOW MOVEMENTS OF HUGER'S DIVISION. 69

It is true that General Johnston modifies this statement by adding: "Unless he found in his front force enough to occupy his division." But giving full weight to this qualification of his first statement, General Johnston has unfairly interpreted the sense of the orders he gave Huger. The latter was positively instructed to make his "progress to the front" "conform at first to that of General Hill." In case he should find no strong body in his front he was *mildly* instructed: "It will be well to aid General Hill; but then a strong reserve should be retained to cover our right."

These instructions say nothing about General Longstreet or his division. At the time they were written General Johnston expected that Longstreet's division would move on the Nine-miles road and go promptly into action, in support of D. H. Hill's division, as soon as the latter attacked the Federals on the Williamsburg road. It was not then intended that Huger, from the Charles City road, should aid Longstreet on the Nine-miles road. But, in "the combined movement which had been planned," General Johnston intended—"should there be cause of haste"—that McLaws's division; on, and north of the Nine-miles road; should re-enforce Longstreet.

It should be noticed that whilst Generals Longstreet and Johnston severely censure the "slowness" of Huger's division, they are silent in regard to the causes of "delay." In his official report to General Johnston, General Longstreet says that "It did not get into position, however, to make any such attack, and I was obliged to send three of my small brigades on the Charles City road" "to protect my right flank;" and he adds: "After waiting some six hours for" Huger's division "to get into position I determined to move forward without regard to them." "I have reason to believe that the affair would have been a complete success had" Huger's division "been put in position within eight hours of the proper time. The want of promptness on that part of the field and the consequent severe struggle in my front so greatly reduced my supply of ammunition, that at the late hour of the move on the left [by the division, under Whiting, on the Nine-miles road] I was unable to make the rush necessary to relieve that attack." "My own troops have been so often tried and distinguished on other fields that they need no praise from my lips. A truer, better body of men never marched upon a battle-field."

The battle of Seven Pines was the first great contest between the Federal Army of the Potomac and the Confederate Army of Northern Virginia. When the two small Confederate armies, under Johnston and Beauregard, contended against the Federals under McDowell at the first battle of Manassas, General Longstreet commanded a Confederate brigade, which, from its position on the field, was not called upon to do any special fighting. In the affair at Williamsburg—between the rear of the Confederates, retiring from Yorktown to the vicinity of Richmond, and the advanced portion of the Federal army—Longstreet's division took an active part in the rather blind fighting in the woods east of the Confederate fortifications; and they did good service there. If his troops had been tried and distinguished on any other fields than those just mentioned, that fact is not generally known.

What he says of his being "obliged to send" three of his brigades on the Charles City road to protect his right flank, and his statement that Huger's "want of promptness" so greatly reduced the "supply of ammunition," will be referred to in another connection.

General Johnston, in his official report, says: The divisions "of Smith, Hill and Longstreet were in position early enough" "to be ready to commence operations by 8 A. M. Major-General Longstreet, unwilling to make a partial attack, instead of the combined movement which had been planned, waited from hour to hour for General Huger's division."

He adds: "Had Major-General Huger's division been in position and ready for action when those of Smith, Longstreet and Hill moved I am satisfied that Keyes's corps would have been destroyed instead of being merely defeated. Had it gone into action even at 4 o'clock, the victory would have been much more complete."

Without discussing here "the combined movement" which Generals Johnston and Longstreet claim required that Huger's

ALLEGED SLOW MOVEMENTS OF HUGER'S DIVISION.   71

division should attack the left flank and rear of the Federals, it may be stated:

The divisions of Smith, Hill and Longstreet were *not* in position early enough to commence operations by 8 A. M.

Smith's division, under Whiting, directed by General Johnston, in person, went into action, against Sumner, north of Fair Oaks Station, at 5 P. M.

Hill's division moved to the attack, on the Williamsburg road, at 1 P. M.*

One brigade of Longstreet's division was put into the fight at 4 P. M. The five other brigades of Longstreet's division were not in action that day.

If Huger's division "did not go into action by 4 o'clock, it was because General Longstreet did not require it, as it was in position and awaiting his orders."

Attention will now be called to the action taken by General

---

* In reference to the hour at which D. H. Hill's division was in "position" "to commence operations," attention is called to the following quotations, in addition to what has already been stated in regard to the time at which the divisions were moved into action. At 6.30 A. M., May 31, General D. H. Hill wrote to General Rodes: "Have your men ready to start at a moment's notice. Examine their cartridge boxes, and if their ammunition be damaged, have it supplied from the ordnance wagons. . . . Carter's battery will move with you. Have a strip of cloth (white) prepared as a battle badge for each man. . . . Specific battle instructions will be given hereafter." See "Official Records," Vol. XI., Part III., p. 564. The date, 6.30 A. M.. of these preparatory instructions, would hardly indicate that Hill's division would be in position "to commence operations" at 8 A. M. But on this point we are not left to "inference." General Rodes in his official report says: "On the morning of the 31st, the brigade was stationed on the Charles City road, three and one-half miles from the point on the Williamsburg road from which it had been determined to start the columns of attack. Between 10 and 11 A. M. I received an order through an officer of Major-General Hill's staff to put my brigade in motion. . . . Finding that the movement of my brigade under this order was premature, with Major-General Hill's approval, I sent a staff officer to remand it to its original position. A short time after this I received a verbal order from General Hill to conduct my command at once to the point at which the attack was to be made. . . . When the signal for attack was given [at 1 P. M.], only my line of skirmishers, the Sixth Alabama, and another regiment, the Twelfth Mississippi, were in position."

Huger soon after the official reports of Generals Longstreet and Johnston were made public.

On the 10th of August, 1862, General Huger made the following indorsement on General Longstreet's official report : *

"I received this day the within report. I applied † for it on July 26, but could not obtain it till this date. It is respectfully returned, with my objections to its being received as the proper report of that battle :

"1st. General Longstreet was not the senior officer present. We met on duty, and I inquired of him if he knew which was the senior, as I did not. He replied that he was. I told him, if he knew it, that was sufficient. But General Longstreet was mistaken, and the statement that he was the senior was erroneous. I was the senior.

"2d. The whole of the remarks of the delay of my division are erroneous. There was a delay owing to the sudden rising of the stream on which the troops were encamped. General Longstreet's division got the road at the crossing first and my troops had to wait until they had passed. The delay after that [at the stream] was the time necessary to cross. I regretted the delay as much as any one and did all in my power to expedite the movement.

"3d. His statement, 'I have reason to believe that the affair would have been a complete success had the troops upon the right [Huger's division] been put in position within eight hours of the proper time,' is a gross error. If the proper time was 4 A. M. the troops were eight hours late, but under the circumstances that was impossible. The 'proper time' is a vague expression. The idea of gross or criminal negligence is conveyed, but not proved. If he had said ' possible time,' there might have been some delay that greater exertion or better management would have avoided, but none other.

"4th. I have applied to General Longstreet to correct the errors he has made, and desire he may have time to do so." ‡

---

* It does not appear that any report of the operations of Huger's division was called for by either General Longstreet or General Johnston. It is believed that no regular official report was made by Huger. G. W. S.

† To the Confederate States War Department.

‡ " Official Records," Vol. XI., Part I., p. 942.

On the 20th of September, 1862, General Huger wrote to General Johnston:

"I beg to refer you to my letter* of the 20th ultimo. I have waited one month, and no reply has been received from General Longstreet. As you have indorsed his erroneous statements, to my injury, I must hold you responsible, and desire to know from you if you have any reason to believe an answer will be made by General Longstreet. You must perceive that by postponing an answer your published report is allowed to go down to history as true. I cannot conceive that you desire to perpetrate such an injustice, for though it may ruin me, it cannot redound to your credit. If you will investigate the case I am sure you will discover the errors of your report and correct them; but if I am thus to suffer by sixty and ninety days' delay, I must claim a court at once. I send you herewith an abstract of such parts of your report as refer to my division, with my remarks annexed, to which I invite your attention." †

In that abstract the quotations already given from General Johnston's report are made by General Huger; and he adds the following "*remarks*":

"Appended hereto are the instructions—two letters from General Johnston to Major-General Huger. [These letters have already been given.] No mention is made in them that General Longstreet had the direction of operations upon the right, and it will be seen from these letters that the plan of attack was not communicated to him [Huger]. He, the senior officer present, was deprived of the position due to his rank and kept in ignorance of the troops he was to act with. General Longstreet's troops were not in position to commence operations by 8 A. M., and General Longstreet makes no mention of the delay [caused] by the rain of the previous night. When General Longstreet's troops moved to support General Hill's attack, General Huger's division [two brigades of it] moved down the Charles City road at the same time with three brigades of General Longstreet's division. This report conveys the impression that the brigades of General Huger's division were not present at all, whereas they [except

---
* Not found in official records.
† "Official Records," Vol. XI., Part I., p. 935.

Mahone's brigade, which for several hours had already been far out on the Charles City road], moved to their position with three brigades of General Longstreet's division. This statement [conveying the impression that Huger's division was not present at all] is not sustained by the above facts. To the last paragraph [quoted from Johnston's report] I have only to say that if it [Huger's division] did not go into action by four o'clock it was because General Longstreet did not require it, as it was in position and awaiting his orders. . . ."*

On the 21st of September, General Huger wrote to President Davis: "I send you herewith an extract of such portions of General J. E. Johnston's published report of the battle of Seven Pines as refer to my division, with my remarks appended. As General Johnston does not seem disposed to investigate the subject, and shields himself by endeavoring to make General Longstreet responsible for his statements, I have to request that you direct General Johnston to prefer charges against me for the negligence he attributes to me, and we then be examined by a court-martial. If this cannot be done, I ask a court of inquiry to examine into the facts. I am entitled to this protection to my reputation and this justice to the troops I command."

On the 28th of September, President Davis placed the following indorsement on the above letter:

"Secretary of War will communicate a copy of this application to General Johnston, that he may, if he chooses to do so, put his statement in the exact form of charges and specifications, and should he decline to adopt that course, the request of General Huger, presented as an alternative, will be granted, and a court of inquiry ordered as soon as the state of the public service will permit."

On the 2d of October the Secretary of War wrote to General Johnston:

"I have the honor to inclose for your attention copies of a letter addressed to the President by General Huger, and of the indorsement made thereon by the President."

To which General Johnston replied on the 4th of October:

---

* "Official Records," Vol. XI., Part I., p. 937.

"I have just had the honor to receive your letter of the 2d instant. I have no disposition to prefer charges against Major-General Huger. The passage in my report of which he complains was written to show that the delay in commencing the action of May 31 was not by my fault. Permit me to suggest that there can be no full investigation of this matter without Major-General Longstreet's participation.

"Major-General Huger's assertion that I 'shield myself by endeavoring to make General Longstreet responsible for my statements' is utterly unfounded. He certainly knows that I cannot contradict that officer's report unless upon the weight of evidence against it. He makes no material contradiction of what I said of his troops. I say or imply that they arrived after 4 P. M.; he, that they reached the 'designated point' before 4 o'clock.

"As to investigation, General Huger knows that his own course has made any other than that which has been had impracticable. He knew that for several weeks after he read my report General Longstreet was near Richmond, yet he did not address me on the subject in question until that officer had joined the army in Northern Virginia. When so addressed I wrote immediately, which General Huger did also. General Longstreet has lately replied to his letter.

"I hope that the President will do me the favor to read the last two paragraphs." *

On the 9th of October, President Davis placed the following indorsement on the above:

"To Secretary of War—It may be that the expected answer of General Longstreet will enable General Johnston to relieve General Huger of the grievance presented by the latter. Should it be otherwise, his request for a court of inquiry will be complied with as soon as the state of the service will permit."

The "expected answer of General Longstreet" is not found; but whatever it may have been, it did not relieve General Huger of the "grievance" to which he was subjected by Generals Longstreet and Johnston. The indorsement placed by President Davis on General Johnston's letter of October 4, 1862, was the

---

* "Official Records," Vol. XI., Part I., p. 938.

last official action in the case. The President did not order the court of inquiry; and the letter of General Johnston, just referred to, was all the " redress " accorded to General Huger, in response to his appeal to President Davis for " protection " against injustice.

The failure—practical refusal—of President Davis to permit a legal investigation in this case resulted in leaving Huger under the very severe censure contained in the published official reports of Generals Longstreet and Johnston. The "papers" in the case remained on file in the Confederate War office—and Huger's statements were not made public until they came out in the " Official Records" published by the United States War Department.

If President Davis had permitted an inquiry to be made by a court of competent jurisdiction, the written instructions given by General Johnston to General Huger would have shown the court that Huger was not ordered " to make a strong flank movement around the left of the enemy's position and attack him in rear of that flank," as stated in the official report of General Longstreet. Those instructions would have shown, too, that General Huger was not ordered " to move down the Charles City road in order to attack in flank the troops who might be engaged with Hill and Longstreet;" as stated in General Johnston's official report. Huger was instructed : " If you find no strong body in your front, it will be well to aid General Hill ; but then a strong reserve should be retained to cover our right."

The court could hardly have failed to find that, whilst Huger was delayed in leaving his camp by a sudden freshet in Gilliss creek; which, at daylight, was a raging torrent; Longstreet's division reached Huger's camp between 7 and 8 A. M., took precedence of Huger's division, and still farther materially delayed the latter. Between 10 and 11 A. M., by authority from General Johnston, Longstreet took control of Huger and of the movements of Huger's division. From that time Huger cheerfully and promptly obeyed every order he received from Longstreet.

After both of these divisions had crossed Gilliss creek, Mahone's brigade, of Huger's division, was sent well out on the

Charles City road, and remained there until June 1. The two other brigades of Huger's division and three brigades of Longstreet's division were retained near the junction of the Charles City and Williamsburg roads until 3.30 P. M. The disposition made of these five brigades by General Longstreet after that time will be described later.

Whilst the facts submitted to President Davis by General Huger lay dormant in the archives of the Confederate War Department; subject to promulgation only by order of the President or by act of Congress; the official reports of Generals Johnston and Longstreet were widely published and "allowed to go down to history as true," notwithstanding Huger's appeal for "protection" to his reputation and "justice" to the troops under his command.

In illustration of the extent to which erroneous statements of Generals Longstreet and Johnston, in regard to Huger's instructions have been incorporated in history, the following quotation is made from the writings of ex-President Davis. Although his attention had been specially called to the instructions given to Huger by General Johnston, it will be found that the ex-President accepts as true General Longstreet's incorrect version of the orders given by General Johnston for the movements of Huger's division. It will be seen, too, that whilst he ignores all that General Huger said in reference to the "delays" and the causes thereof, the ex-President introduces explanations and excuses for Huger's "dilatoriness" that have little or no foundation. In attempting, at this late day, to exonerate General Huger, the ex-President differs from Generals Johnston and Longstreet. He offers "some explanation," whilst they adhere to their unqualified censure.

Ex-President Davis says:* "The reference made without qualification, in General Longstreet's report, to the failure of General Huger to make the attack expected of him . . . renders it proper that some explanation should be given of an apparent dilatoriness on the part of that veteran soldier. . . . .

---

* See "Rise and Fall of the Confederate Government," Vol. II., p. 125. Published 1881.

It will be remembered that General Huger was to move by the Charles City road, so as to turn the left of the enemy and attack him in flank. The extraordinary rain of the previous night had swollen every rivulet to the dimensions of a stream, and the route prescribed to General Huger was one especially affected by that heavy rain, as it led to the head of the White Oak Swamp. The bridge over the stream flowing into that swamp had been carried away, and the alternative presented to him was to rebuild the bridge or leave his artillery. He chose the former, which involved the delay that has subjected him to criticism. If any should think an excuse necessary to justify this decision, they are remanded to the accepted military maxim, that the march must never be so hurried as to arrive unfit for service. . . . To show that the obstacles encountered were not of such slight character as energy would readily overcome, I refer to the report of . . . Brigadier-General Rodes."

The latter commanded a brigade of D. H. Hill's division, in observation on the Charles City road, three and one-half miles from the point on the Williamsburg road from which it had been determined to start D. H. Hill's columns of attack. Mr. Davis quotes Rodes's report: "'The progress of the brigade was considerably delayed by the washing away of a bridge near the head of White Oak Swamp, by reason of which the men had to wade in water waist deep, and a large number were entirely submerged. At this point the character of the crossing was such that it was absolutely necessary to proceed with great caution to prevent the loss of both ammunition and life.'"

Mr. Davis adds: "General Huger's line of march was further to the right, therefore nearer to White Oak Swamp, and the impediments consequently greater than where General Rodes found the route so difficult as to be dangerous even to infantry."

The only stream that delayed Huger's movements was Gilliss creek, on the banks of which his division was encamped on the night of the 30th, near the eastern suburb of Richmond, not far north of the point where the Williamsburg road leaves the city. Gilliss creek flows into James river within the city limits. The accounts make no reference to the washing away or the rebuilding of a bridge for the passage of artillery over that stream.

The causes of delay at this crossing, and the movements of Huger's division, previous to 3.30 p. m., have already been stated. It is now proposed to show, from the official record, the disposition made of Huger's division by General Longstreet after that time. It will be borne in mind that Mahone's brigade of Huger's division had already been sent out on the Charles City road to the point previously occupied by Rodes's brigade, and remained there until June 1. Mahone's orders were "to cover our right" and guard against the approach of the enemy, on that road, from the White Oak Bridge. Huger's division was composed of three brigades only. There are two brigades still to be accounted for.

General Cadmus M. Wilcox commanded three of the six brigades of which Longstreet's division was composed. In his official report to General Longstreet General Wilcox, after stating that his command was halted near the junction of the Williamsburg and Charles City roads until 3.30 p. m., adds:

"I was then ordered to move with three brigades, my own, Colston's and Pryor's, on the Charles City road, in rear of a part of Huger's division (Blanchard's and Armistead's brigades) as a support to these troops; this order was soon modified and my three brigades ordered to precede Huger's. Having passed Huger's brigades, the march was continued but a short time, when orders were again received, and this time to countermarch to the Williamsburg road and follow on in rear of the troops then advancing. The brigades had retraced their steps near one mile, and orders were again given to face about and march down the Charles City road, and to keep abreast with the firing then heard raging furiously off to our left front, and known to be on the Williamsburg road. Again orders were received in writing to move across to the Williamsburg road, following country roads and paths through woods and fields, a guide being furnished to conduct the command. The intervening distance between the two roads was low and flat, and in many places covered with water, and at one point waist-deep. The march was of necessity very slow. It was about 5 p. m. when the head of the column reached the Williamsburg road."

General Wilcox's report shows farther that only three companies of the leading regiment of these five brigades reached the front in time to take part in the fighting. The remainder of this column of five brigades, from the Charles City road, under Longstreet's orders, were not in close action that day. Three of these brigades were in Longstreet's own division; and, by his order, they had been placed in front of Huger's two brigades.

From General Wilcox's report it is seen that the route followed by Huger's troops from the Charles City road to the Williamsburg road was to the *left* of that by which Rodes's brigade marched to its position in D. H. Hill's line of battle; not to the *right* of Rodes's route, as stated by Mr. Davis. It is also clear that the whole "bridge scene," as described by Mr. Davis, including the "alternative" and his application of the "accepted military maxim," are fictions of imagination. Whereas, Huger's proper and complete defense against the severe censure to which he has been so long unjustly subjected, is found in well established facts, many of which were plainly stated in the documents which accompanied his application to President Davis for the appointment of a court of inquiry.

General Longstreet's letter, June 7, 1862, addressed to General Johnston, seems to be the germ from which the official censure of General Huger was evolved. In that letter Longstreet says: "Our ammunition was nearly exhausted when Whiting moved, and I could not therefore move on with the rush that we could had his movement been earlier." When Longstreet's note, complaining of Johnston's slowness, in moving Whiting, was written, not one of the six brigades in Longstreet's division had been put in action. Eight of the thirteen brigades under Longstreet's control were not put into the fight that day. Yet, he would have it believed that before 4 P. M. his ammunition was so nearly exhausted, "I could not, therefore, move on with the rush that we could."

He adds: "I can't but help think that a display of his forces on the left flank of the enemy by General Huger would have completed the affair and given Whiting as easy and pretty a game as was ever had upon a battle-field." It is not quite clear that a "display" of Huger's "forces," in the impracticable White Oak Swamp, "on the left flank of the enemy," would have "given Whiting an easy and pretty game," with Sumner north of Fair

Oaks Station. But, if General Longstreet had then really believed the " display " he speaks of would have " completed the affair,"— including Sumner, and such Federal re-enforcements as might be sent from the north side of the Chickahominy—all that General Longstreet would have had to do, in order to test this matter, was to direct Huger to make that " display." Huger's division " was in position and awaiting " Longstreet's " orders."

But the " display " theory, promulgated by General Longstreet on the 7th of June, is not in accord with his action on the 31st of May, in placing three brigades of his own division on the Charles City road, in order to protect his right flank, and marching and counter-marching these three brigades and two brigades of Huger's division up and down that road, near its junction with the Williamsburg road, whilst D. H. Hill's four brigades, aided only by one brigade of Longstreet's division, were desperately contending with superior forces in fortified position near Seven Pines.

But it seems that what Longstreet said in his letter of June 7, and in his official report, June 10, in regard to Huger's division, was accepted by General Johnston as sufficient to prove that the " slow movements of General Huger's command " was the real cause of the failure of the Confederates to destroy Keyes's corps on the 31st of May. This, too, when Johnston knew that five brigades of Longstreet's own division were not put in action that day, and that Huger was under Longstreet's control!

In making up their respective official reports, Generals Johnston and Longstreet gave no hearing to Huger in regard to the operations of his division; and when Huger appealed to General Johnston for justice, the latter adhered to all that he had said in censure of Huger—declined to investigate the subject—discouraged inquiry by a court—and said: " The passage in my report of which he complains was written to show that the delay in commencing the action of May 31 was not by my fault "!

If General Johnston had then permitted the fact to be " generally known " that Longstreet " misunderstood " the direction in which his own division was to move into action, there would have been no occasion to say more in order to prove that this " misunderstanding " caused " delay in commencing the action May 31."

Instead of saying: "Had" Huger's division "gone into action even at 4 o'clock the victory would have been more complete;" General Johnson might well have said: *Had Longstreet put his whole division into action, even at 4 o'clock, Keyes's corps would have been destroyed and the victory over McClellan's left wing would have been complete.*

In spite of Longstreet's letter of June 7, and his official report, and the official report of General Johnston, and all that has been said and written by both of them in censure of Huger and Huger's division, the facts, now established, show, beyond doubt, that General Longstreet should be held responsible, under General Johnston, for the failure of the Confederates to destroy Keyes's corps at Seven Pines, on the 31st of May, 1862.

CHAPTER IV.

Contest North of Fair Oaks Station, May 31.

The practical relation which this action bore to the fighting that day on the Williamsburg road, by D. H. Hill's division and R. H. Anderson's brigade of Longstreet's division, was, that the Federal re-enforcements, from the north side of the Chickahominy, did not reach their friends who were beaten in the vicinity of Seven Pines. Moreover, four regiments of infantry and a battery of artillery of Couch's division were cut off from the rest of that division and were not engaged against Longstreet.

In addition, this contest, incidentally prevented one brigade of Kearney's division from joining Keyes at a very critical time for the latter. The foregoing results were obtained by four brigades of the division under Whiting; General Johnston having sent the other brigade of that division direct to the assistance of General Longstreet, who was then supposed to have met with greater opposition than the three divisions under his control could well overcome.

Federal Accounts.—General McClellan, in his official report, says: "As soon as firing was heard at headquarters, orders were sent to General Sumner to get his command under arms and be ready to move at a moment's warning. . . . At 1 o'clock General Sumner moved the two divisions to their respective bridges, with instructions to halt and await further orders. At 2 o'clock orders were sent from headquarters to cross these divisions without delay and push them rapidly to General Heintzelman's support. This order was received and communicated at 2.30 o'clock, and the passage was immediately commenced."

General Sumner, in his official report, says: "At 1 P. M., while stationed with my *corps d'armee* at Tyler's, I received an order from the commanding general to be in readiness to move at a moment's notice. . . . At 2.30 o'clock P. M., I received the order to cross the river and support Heintzelman. The columns immediately moved over the river and marched rapidly to the field. . . . On arriving on the field I found General Couch with four regiments and two companies of infantry and Brady's battery. The troops were drawn up in line near Adams's house, and there was a pause in the battle."

General Sedgwick, in his official report, says: "Upon debouching into the open field, near Adams's house, we found Abercrombie's brigade, of Couch's division, sustaining a severe attack and hard pushed by the enemy."

General Couch, in his official report, after stating that "in twenty minutes" from the time Rippey and Neill were cut up, the enemy had passed over the road leading to his centre, cutting off the advance at Fair Oaks, adds: "At this moment Captain Van Ness, brigade quartermaster to General Abercrombie [the commander of the troops guarding the depot of supplies at Fair Oaks Station], volunteered to notify General Sumner of our situation. After making demonstrations to cut through and rejoin the main body, it was abandoned as suicidal. At the same time large masses of the enemy were moving across the railroad to the front and right with the intention of inclosing us. Therefore, with General Abercrombie, four regiments, the battery and [thirty-five] prisoners, we moved off toward the Grapevine Bridge for half a mile, and took a position facing Fair Oaks. Soon Captain Van Ness brought me word that General Sumner was at hand. Upon receiving the information, word was sent to Generals Heintzelman and Keyes, that my position would be held until General Sumner arrived. This noble soldier came on rapidly with Sedgwick's division, and when the head of his column was seen half a mile distant, I felt that God was with us and victory ours."

General Birney, in his official report, says: "Captain Brady, of the artillery, now rode up to me and said that he came from General Couch, who sent word that his command had been cut off; that he had found a road by which to extricate his artillery through the swamp, and if I could hold the railroad and prevent the enemy from cutting him off, he could extricate himself. I sent him word that I had been sent to his support, and would and could hold the railroad. At this time (about 6 o'clock) Captain Suydam, of General Keyes's staff, rode up to me and told me that General Heintzelman ordered me to advance still up the railroad. . . . I at once made disposition to move forward. . . . When my lines reached the woods near Fair Oaks Station, an oblique artillery fire from the right across my front commenced. To advance would have subjected me to this fire, and supposing that it was General Sumner who had crossed and was advancing, I sent successively three aides to report to him my position [and] instructions, and to ask orders. The orders from him were to connect with General French, commanding his left, and advance *pari passu*. He also sent the Seventh Massachusetts, Colonel Russell, to report to me in order to strengthen my command, as the position held by me was important."

French's brigade did not reach the field until after dark. Birney's brigade was not in action that day; but there can be no reasonable doubt that it would have taken part in the fighting against Colonel Jenkins's forces late that afternoon but for the fact that Couch was held cut off by the Confederates, under Whiting, who advanced on the Nine-miles road.

General Abercrombie, after stating that he fell back about half a mile north of the station, says that he "formed line of battle, the Thirty-first Pennsylvania [on the west of the road] nearest the house, behind a low rail fence, in the rear of a piece of woods. Two companies of the Sixty-first Pennsylvania and First United States Chasseurs [Sixty-fifth New York Infantry] were posted on the right of the Thirty-first Pennsylvania. The other troops on the ground at the time were the Sixty-second New York and Seventh Massachusetts, and a section of Brady's battery, formed on the left [east] of the road. The other section of Brady's battery was placed on the right of my command."

General Sedgwick says: "The First Minnesota, Colonel Sully, the leading regiment, was, by request of General Couch, approved by General Sumner, promptly formed into line of battle under a very sharp fire, and posted on the right of Abercrombie's brigade. . . . The remainder of Gorman's brigade, led by him in person, and composed of the Thirty-fourth and Eighty-second New

York, supported by the Fifteenth Massachusetts, formed on the left of Abercrombie's brigade. . . . Lieutenant Kirby brought his battery into action in a most gallant and spirited manner. . . . Generals Burns and Dana were promptly on hand—the former with his whole brigade, the latter with two of his regiments. . . . General Dana with the two regiments . . . was ordered to form in column of attack to the rear and left of Kirby's battery, but before the order could be executed it became necessary to push him to the front, where he went immediately into action on the left of Gorman's brigade. . . . General Burns with two regiments took post on the right of Colonel Sully, holding his other two in reserve. It was not the fortune of any of the regiments in this brigade to meet the enemy [that day] at close quarters."

Lieutenant-Colonel Nevin, commanding the Sixty-second New York, of Peck's brigade, states that the regiment marched from Couch's line at Seven Pines to Fair Oaks Station. He describes a movement from that point to feel the enemy approaching on the railroad, and adds: "We were then ordered to move up the road leading north from the station to a clump of woods. . . . We discovered the enemy emerging from the woods on the west of us. . . . They filed along the railroad to the open space, when the enemy formed in line of battle, advanced at double-quick, when our late Colonel ordered the regiment to file out of the woods by the left flank. As soon as the enemy saw our colors they opened fire upon our regiment. We were immediately formed in line of battle by the Colonel to the rear of Ricketts's[*] and Brady's batteries. Shortly after forming in line, Colonel J. Lafayette Riker was killed while gallantly cheering on his men to save the battery."

This regiment remained in support of the battery until the action ended. There seems to have been no official report of that day's operations made by Colonel Russell, the commander of the Seventh Massachusetts, of Devens's brigade. It supported the batteries until sent by General Sumner to aid General Birney on the railroad. Two regiments of Burns's brigade remained in position, supporting the batteries until the action was over.

---

[*] Commanded by Lieutenant Edmund Kirby.

The official reports of the Federal general officers give great credit to the artillery in this action. Lieutenant Edmund Kirby, commanding Light Battery I, First United States Artillery, says: "I was ordered by General Sumner to place the battery [six pieces] in position, the right resting on a strip of woods and the left about seventy yards from Adams's house, facing nearly south and toward Fair Oaks Station. The enemy advanced through an open field, and were about 1,000 yards from the battery when I commenced firing with spherical case and shell. They immediately tried to cover themselves in the woods on my right. . . . I ordered shell and spherical case to be fired until the enemy were within 500 yards of my right flank, when I opened with canister. The enemy now prepared to charge my right. I advanced the left of the battery. They came down a road which was on my right when the firing commenced, and when they emerged from the woods found themselves directly in front of the battery instead of on the right, as they expected, and were consequently subjected to a tremendous fire of canister from five * light twelve-pounder guns, which they were unable to stand. They retreated in disorder into the woods. . . . During the entire action the enemy kept up a continuous fire of musketry upon us, but fortunately most of their balls too high, as the caissons and limbers were well covered by an elevation upon which the pieces were placed. During the battle I made a complete change of front to the right, and at no time had more than five pieces engaged. . . . I claim that we are indebted in no small extent for the success of the day to the personal bravery and efficiency of the officers, non-commissioned officers, and privates of Light Company I, First Artillery."

Captain James Brady, Battery H, First Pennsylvania Reserve Artillery, in his official report, says: "The left section . . . was particularly noticed for the rapidity and effectiveness of its fire, repulsing the head of the enemy's column as it frequently appeared emerging from the wood charging on the battery. This section, after exhausting canister, played upon the enemy's lines with spherical case and shell without fuse, bursting the shell

---

* "In the meantime one trail had broken after the fourth discharge, rendering the piece useless." See Kirby's report.

as it left the gun. . . . The right section, held under my immediate command, moved down to support the centre in time to check a charge of the enemy in that direction, and was, the next moment, ordered to the support of Colonel Sully, First Minnesota. . . . We opened, throwing shell and spherical case without fuse, exploding in the enemy's lines and crushing his flank, causing them to retire, leaving their dead and wounded officers and soldiers on the field."

General Burns, in his official report, says: "Before my brigade had completely formed, the enemy opened on the right of the first line. I received an order from General Sedgwick to throw two of my regiments perpendicularly to the right [these regiments faced nearly west] to prevent the enemy from turning our right flank and getting to our line of communications, which they seemed inclined to do. . . . Night approaching and the enemy being driven back [in his attack on the batteries] the battle ceased."

Colonel Sully, commanding the First Minnesota, Gorman's brigade, in his official report, says: "On reaching the field of action, I found . . . that General Couch's division were hard pressed by an overwhelming force of the rebels. I here met the latter general, and was informed by him that the enemy in strong force were marching to outflank him on the right, and as I was ahead of the rest of the division some distance, not waiting for the commander of my troops, I moved rapidly to the right, about a quarter of a mile; . . . and charging across the field, took my position in an oblique direction, my right resting on a farm-house, my left on the edge of a woods. The enemy opened on us, but fired too high. Soon after the First Chasseurs [Sixty-fifth New York], formed on my left. . . . The enemy left the field in front, and forming in the woods on my left, opened a severe fire on us. . . . Two pieces were sent late in the evening to my assistance, under command of Captain Brady, and did good execution." Colonel Sully's regiment faced nearly west.

Colonel John Cochrane, Sixty-fifth New York, says: "By order of General Abercrombie, the regiment took position in front of a belt of woods through which the enemy's forces were approaching. Our right rested on the left of Colonel Sully's Minnesota regiment, and our left on the right of the Thirty-first Pennsylvania. The men took their places immediately behind the rail fence by which the wood was skirted, and the enemy coming in sight, opened their fire upon them at about twenty-five yards distance. The fire continued two and a half hours, and until the enemy was effectually repulsed. During this time the fire of the men was steady, continuous and accurate, as I have reason to suppose from the very numerous dead found subsequently in the front of our lines. . . . The regiment slept on their arms that night in their position." Colonel Cochrane's regiment and the regiment on his left faced nearly south.

Colonel Williams, commanding the Thirty-first Pennsylvania, says: " We were posted in a well-chosen position behind a low rail fence, an open field in our rear and a wood in front, when the enemy appeared so suddenly and with such impetuosity that our skirmishers could scarcely regain their position in the battalion. The enemy first opened fire, but was met with such a withering volley that his next attempt was made with more caution and deliberation but no better success. His ranks were renewed with fresh troops, which repeatedly charged to within twenty yards of our lines, but no valor or impetuosity could withstand the steady and well-directed fire of our men. As the enemy withdrew to form his shattered lines our fire was slackened, to be renewed with undiminished severity as he approached. The conflict was sustained for nearly two hours, when the enemy withdrew on the approach of night. . . . Our men slept upon their arms in the ranks where the battle had been fought."

General Gorman says: " The Thirty-fourth New York, Fifteenth Massachusetts and Eighty-second New York were formed upon the left of a portion of General Couch's position and Kirby's battery. . . . We had not remained longer than ten minutes in position before heavy columns of the enemy dashed heavily upon us, evidently attempting to take Kirby's battery. . . . The engagement became general from one end of our line to the other, the enemy pushing forward with the most wonderful determination, while I steadily advanced the brigade, from time to time, until we came to a distance of fifty yards, when General Sumner (being present with my brigade) directed me to charge the enemy with the bayonet. . . . The men threw themselves at double-quick headlong upon the enemy, the Thirty-fourth New York somewhat in the advance on the left and in perfect line, the Eighty-second New York on the right, the Fifteenth Massachusetts supporting the centre. I halted the Eighty-second New York and Fifteenth Massachusetts before they entered the woods, but the Thirty-fourth New York plunged into the thicket some fifty paces before I could halt them. A further advance would have imperiled their left flank."

Lieutenant-Colonel Hudson, commanding the Eighty-second New York, says : " In company with the Thirty-fourth [New York], we were at once marched double-quick to support the battery [Kirby's] and took our position with the battery on our right, the Thirty-fourth on our left. At this time the enemy had charged to within about forty or fifty rods of the battery, and received a most terrific fire from my command, which evidently staggered him and caused him to fall back with heavy loss. Again and again did he renew his efforts to take our position, but every time repulsed with heavy loss. In company with the Thirty-fourth New York and Fifteenth Massachusetts we pressed forward, firing as we advanced, and finally drove him from the field at the point of the bayonet, and darkness closing about us, we rested on our arms, the Fifteenth Massachusetts advancing in front of us on the edge of the timber when the enemy had retreated."

Colonel Suiter, Thirty-fourth New York, says, " We arrived on this field about 5.30 P. M. I immediately formed my command in line, its right near the house on the high ground and extending thence easterly along a post-and-rail fence toward the wood in that direction ; . . . about this time we heard volleys of musketry on the westerly side of the house. I was ordered to forward in line over the fence and then formed on the right into line. While I was executing the last-mentioned movement the right of my line received heavy volleys of musketry from the direction of the woods on the west side of the house, which was returned by my command as it arrived on the line. The Eighty-second New York wheeled into line on my right, its right resting upon and supporting the battery, its left on my right. The firing became general along the whole line and continued so for some time; the enemy several times emerged from the woods, evidently with the intention of charging upon and capturing the guns above mentioned, but were as often repulsed and driven back. About 7.30 o'clock the enemy were seen to file out of the woods on the west, evidently with the intention of outflanking and turning our left. About this time the Twentieth Massachusetts [of Dana's brigade] wheeled into line in continuation of ours and on our left. A few well-directed volleys repulsed the enemy at this point and drove them back under cover of the woods ; about a quarter of 8 o'clock I was ordered to charge the enemy with the bayonet in the woods, which they [his regiment] did in good order, pouring into them a withering and deadly fire as they charged, the enemy standing their ground till my command mounted the fence on the skirt of the woods, when they broke and ran in great confusion ; we followed them about twenty rods when we lost sight of them in the darkness ; I was ordered to withdraw my command, which I did, and formed it in the field just outside of the woods, where we rested for the night."

Lieutenant-Colonel Kimball, commanding the Fifteenth Massachusetts, says, " I arrived on the field about 5 o'clock. . . . I immediately formed line of battle in rear of the Eighty-second New York. I had scarcely given the order to rest when a sharp fire of musketry commenced upon Kirby's battery, stationed a short distance to my right ; I was ordered to go to the support of that battery. . . . I immediately formed line of battle in rear of that battery, and remained in that position some time. . . . I was ordered to move by the left flank and to come into the rear and left of the Eighty-second New York, and then to move forward at double-quick, passing their line to the front, and to occupy and hold the wood from which the enemy were being driven. My orders were promptly obeyed, the men charging bayonets into the woods with a terrific yell. I established my line by your command near the edge of the wood, throwing out pickets in front. The men rested upon their arms until morning."

General Dana says, upon reaching the field with the Seventh Michigan and Twentieth Massachusetts, "I received an order from you [Sedgwick] to form my command in columns of divisions in rear of Kirby's battery. . . . I was carrying this order into execution when I received one from General Sumner to form in line of battle, and immediately afterward an order to prolong the first line of battle, already formed, by extending on the left of it, and immediately to engage the enemy."

Gorman's line, the left of which Dana was to prolong, was then facing nearly west, its right near Kirby's battery. General Dana adds: "No sooner was my position taken in line [on the left of Gorman] than I discovered the rebel force in a slight valley in front, where he found a little cover, extending his right so as to outflank our force, and my arrival was not a moment too early. After replying to his first volley, I immediately advanced at double-quick, dislodging him and compelling him to take to cover of woods about 150 yards in his rear. Halting a moment to reform my line, I advanced again to force him through the woods with the bayonet. We received only a scattering fire from him until we came within fifty yards of the wood (it being then dark) when we were again met with a full volley. At this time I compelled the Seventh Michigan, which was on the left, to cease its fire, changed its front a little to meet a corresponding change of the enemy, and then ordered a fire by company, which was well executed in volleys. This closed the action for the day, and we lay on our arms where we stood for the night."

Colonel Lee, of the Twentieth Massachusetts, says: "Conducted by a brigade staff officer we proceeded to the left, where the battalion came into line of battle, forming on the right of the Michigan Seventh. . . . We opened a rapid and effective fire, maintained only a few moments . . . when, in compliance with orders from General Dana, simultaneously with the infantry battalion on our right [the Thirty-fourth New York], and the Michigan Seventh on our left, the line rushed forward with loud cheers. . . . It was now getting quite dark and the enemy soon ceased firing. . . . We occupied the field on which we halted after the last movement to the front, all night under arms, engaged mainly in securing prisoners and collecting and providing as best we could for the enemy's wounded, who were numerous, and scattered on the field around us." Among the wounded prisoners he mentions Brigadier-General Pettigrew.

Thus, the Federal accounts show that the fighting continued until dark, at which time Kirby's battery faced west instead of south, without having otherwise changed position during the action. The three regiments of Gorman's brigade, which were in the beginning on the left of the batteries, and facing south, now faced nearly west, their right being still on the left of the batteries. Dana's two regiments prolonged Gorman's line, and extended nearly to the railroad a little east of Fair Oaks Station. The two regiments that were on the right of Kirby's battery, and facing nearly south when the action commenced, had not changed position. Sully's regiment and two of Burns's were still on the right, facing nearly west.

The Federal losses on this field were 468. Of which 342 were in Sedgwick's division, viz.: Gorman's brigade, 196; Burns's brigade, 35, and Dana's brigade, 111. In the four "cut-off" regiments of Couch's division, 115; and in the two batteries, 11.

From the foregoing, it is clear that the opportune arrival of Federal re-enforcements under Sumner, from the north side of the Chickahominy, at a point about 1,000 yards north of Fair Oaks Station, saved Couch's four regiments and battery. But these re-enforcements did not reach Heintzelman and Keyes, by whom they were so greatly needed when Kearney was forced to retreat through the White Oak Swamp, and Heintzelman and Keyes were desperately contending against Colonel Jenkins until dark, on the Williamsburg road, east of Seven Pines. These re-enforcements, being thus prevented from joining the friends they were sent to aid, the question arises: What would have been the probable result to Heintzelman and Keyes—who were badly beaten by five brigades—if Longstreet had promptly put into the fight the five brigades of his own division, which were not in action that day.

Confederate Accounts.—It is greatly to be regretted that neither General Whiting, nor any of the brigade or regimental commanders under him, made a report in regard to the operations of their respective commands. The circumstances under which my official report was made have already been stated.

When General Johnston hurriedly left his headquarters near Old Tavern to direct the movement from that point "against the right flank of Longstreet's adversaries," he ordered me to have Hampton's and Hatton's brigades brought up at once, and immediately follow the three leading brigades. I was soon informed that Hampton and Hatton were in motion. I then joined Generals Johnston and Whiting in the advance. At that time the troops had just passed McLaws's pickets, and were receiving the fire of the Federal skirmish line, from rifle-pits in the edge of the woods, on the eastern side of the large open field. General Johnston had ordered Hood's brigade to bear to the right and go direct to Longstreet's assistance; whilst Whiting's brigade and Pettigrew's continued along, and on either side of, the Nine-miles road. I remained with Generals Johnston and Whiting in rear of the leading brigade, Whiting's, until we reached a point on the Nine-miles road about three-fourths of a mile from Fair Oaks Station, from which a wood road branched off towards the north. I remained at that point until the rear of Pettigrew's brigade passed me. From that time I did not see either General Johnston or General Whiting until after dark.

The former, in his official report, says: "Major-General Smith's division moved forward at 4 o'clock, Whiting's three brigades leading. Their progress was impeded by the enemy's skirmishers, which, with their supports, were driven back to the railroad. At this point Whiting's own and Pettigrew's brigades engaged a superior force of the enemy; Hood's, by my order, moved on to co-operate with Longstreet. General Smith was desired to hasten up with all the troops within reach. He brought up Hampton's and Hatton's brigades in a few minutes. The strength of the enemy's position, however, enabled him to hold it until dark. About sunset, being struck from my horse severely wounded by a fragment of a shell, I was carried from the field, and Major-General G. W. Smith succeeded to the command."

In the *Century Magazine*, May, 1885, General Johnston says: "On my way to Longstreet's left, to combine the action of the two bodies of troops, I passed the head of General Smith's column near Fair Oaks, and saw the camps of about a brigade in the angle between the Nine-miles road and the York River Railroad, and the rear of a column of infantry moving in quick time from that point towards the Chickahominy, by the road to Grapevine ford. A few minutes after this, a battery near the point where this infantry had disappeared commenced firing upon the head of the Confederate column. A regiment sent against it was received with a volley of musketry, as well as canister, and recoiled. The leading brigade, commanded by Colonel Law, then advanced, and so much strength was developed by the enemy that General Smith brought his other brigades into action on the left of Law's. An obstinate contest began, and was maintained on equal terms, although we engaged superior numbers on ground of their own choosing. I had passed the railroad a few hundred yards with Hood's brigade when the firing commenced, and stopped to see it terminated. But being confident that the enemy opposing us were those whose camp I had just seen, and therefore only a brigade, I did not doubt that General Smith was more than strong enough to cope with them. Therefore, General Hood was directed to go on in such a direction as to connect his right with Longstreet's left and take his antagonists in flank. The direction of that firing was then nearly southwest from Fair Oaks. It was then about 5 o'clock. . . . It was nearly half-past 6 o'clock before I admitted to myself that Smith was engaged, not with a brigade, as I had obstinately thought, but with more than a division; but I thought that it would be injudicious to engage Magruder's division, our only reserve, so late in the day."

It is not deemed necessary to comment here upon what General Johnston says about "Smith's column": "General Smith brought his other brigades into action;" "I did not doubt that General Smith was more than strong enough to cope with them;" " it was near half-past 6 o'clock before I admitted to myself that Smith was engaged, not with a brigade;" and like expressions, conveying the distinct impression that I was that day in executive command of the division which bore my name.

The following testimony of Captain George Lemmon,* Vol-

---

* In a letter dated San Francisco, April 12, 1884, addressed to me. G. W. S.

unteer Aide-de-Camp to General Hood, is of interest in connection with the events of that afternoon. He says that when Hood's brigade, moving along the railroad, was closely approaching Fair Oaks Station, they " saw troops in front," " on the left, moving in the same direction." " General Hood ordered me to see what troops they were; and, if they were our men, to tell them not to fire into his brigade. As I got to them General Hood passed me, his horse at full gallop, and called out 'I am General Hood. Who are you?' And they answered, 'Third Brigade, General.' He said, 'All right; don't fire into my men.'" The third brigade was Whiting's own.

Captain Lemmon's testimony shows that, in the vicinity of Fair Oaks Station, Hood's brigade was again close on the right of Whiting's. It was from that position Hood was again directed by General Johnston " to go on " and " connect his right with Longstreet's left." Whilst Hood was moving under this order, the two wings of his brigade became separated—Colonel Archer of the Fifth Texas and another regiment getting separated from the two that were left with General Hood, with whom Captain Lemmon remained. He adds: " We pushed on . . . until we came to an open space where we found Colonel Archer with two regiments and several brigades, standing still in front of us in the same open space. General Hood asked, 'What troops are those?' and Archer replied, 'D. H. Hill's.'[*] Hood said, 'There is no use for us here; . . . Captain Lemmon, take the First Texas and lead off to the left.' Colonel Rainey of the First Texas asked, 'What shall I do if I am fired on?' Hood replied, 'Face to the firing and go in where it is heaviest; you can make no mistake then.' . . . An order was passed from the right of the line to return. . . . I found myself in the woods with darkness fast growing, under heavy fire and wounded men coming out who belonged to Whiting's brigade. Staying there until the firing ceased, I called for Colonel Rainey, when he arose some ten or fifteen feet from me. I asked him why he had not advanced to the firing; and he told me he had done so, but other

---

[*] These were the brigades of G. B. Anderson and Garland, that had been withdrawn from the second abatis and reformed in the clearing, and " after night " were ordered to take position in the woods west of the first abatis.

troops arose between him and the enemy and he ordered his men down, not knowing but the enemy were firing into each other and not caring if they were. I told him that it was the Third Brigade in front of him and then led him back to General Hood. . . . We then crossed the railroad and returned to the north side and laid the men down until General Whiting ordered Hood to move his men to the right, placing one regiment across the railroad."

When Hood reached the edge of the open space around Casey's redoubt, D. H. Hill's troops had retired from the second abatis and Colonel Jenkins was fighting the right of "Longstreet's antagonists," on the Williamsburg road, east of Seven Pines. When Hood again reached Fair Oaks, it was about dark, and Whiting's brigade had just been beaten back. In fighting qualities Hood's brigade was equal to any in the Confederate Army. It is not proposed to speculate at any length upon what would have been the probable result of the contest north of Fair Oaks, if General Johnston had been less "obstinate" in the opinion that "Smith" was only contending with "a brigade"; and had not ordered Hood from Fair Oaks Station "to go on," and in such a direction as to "connect his right with Longstreet's left." If Hood had been recalled earlier, he would have come upon the field before dark; in position to fall in full force upon Dana's left flank; and would have materially disturbed the equanimity with which the five regiments that charged Whiting just before dark, laid on their arms that night.

In reference to the attack Whiting made upon the batteries north of Fair Oaks, Colonel Frobel, in his letter to me, previously quoted, says: "Generals Johnston and Whiting were following immediately after Whiting's brigade. As Whiting's brigade reached the road near the railroad crossing, I was sent to halt it. On returning after doing this, I joined Generals Johnston and Whiting, who were riding toward the crossing. General Whiting was expostulating with General Johnston about taking the division across the railroad—insisting that the enemy were in full force on our left flank and rear. General Johnston replied 'Oh! General Whiting, you are too cautious.' At this time we reached the crossing and nearly at the same moment the enemy opened an artillery fire from the direction pointed out by General Whiting. We moved back up the road near the small white house. Whiting's brigade was gone—it had been ordered forward to charge the batteries which were firing on us. The brigade was repulsed, and in a few moments came streaming back through the little skirt of woods to the left of the Nine-miles road near the crossing. There was only a part of the brigade in this charge. Pender soon rallied and reformed those on the edge of the woods. General Whiting sent an order to him to reconnoiter the batteries, and if he thought they could be taken to try it again. Before he could do so some one galloped up, shouting 'charge that battery!' The men moved forward at a double-quick, but were repulsed as before, and driven back to the woods. In the meantime there was heavy fighting going on to the left; Hatton's, Hampton's and Pettigrew's brigades having engaged the enemy in that direction. At this moment matters had become so critical on that portion of the field that, although not commanding the division, you had gone to Hampton's and Hatton's brigades and taken a personal supervision over their immediate line of battle. Hampton was wounded, Pettigrew wounded and a prisoner, and Hatton killed, and his brigade much demoralized. At this time I was ordered to bring up Hood. I found him to the right of the railroad, a little to the left of the Williamsburg road and not a great way from Seven Pines. By the time he reached the position indicated on the left of the railroad it was nearly dark. I joined General Whiting and yourself in the little oat-field where the battle began, and about 200 yards from the place where General Johnston was wounded. Whiting's brigade still held the wood where [from which] they had made their first charge, and so did Hampton's, Hatton's and Pettigrew's brigades. You immediately set about reforming our lines."

In my official, published, report it is stated that:

" Between 4 and 5 o'clock heavy musketry was distinctly heard [by those near Old Tavern], and General Johnston directed General Whiting to move the three brigades then at that point by the Nine-miles road to Longstreet's assistance and the two brigades at Mrs. Christian's farm were ordered to move up, follow, and support them. All the generals and staff officers were at once occupied in impressing upon the troops the necessity of moving rapidly forward. . . . The troops, notwithstanding the mud and difficulties of the ground, moved forward in double-quick time; . . . only anxious to find the enemy in force, who were still making resistance in front of Longstreet and Hill. Hood's brigade had crossed the railroad to the right of the Nine-miles road, part of Whiting's had also crossed, Pettigrew close upon it, with Hatton's and Hampton's a short distance in rear, when a fire from two batteries of artillery opened upon the advance brigade from a position on their left and rear. These batteries were supported by infantry, and the fire becoming troublesome, it was determined to take them, at the same time not giving up the forward movement in favor of Longstreet. . . . I received from General Johnston instructions to move all the troops within reach forward as fast as possible. This order was at once transmitted to General Magruder, who caused all his troops [Griffith's brigade and two regiments] in that vicinity to be put in motion. General Johnston was at this time near the point where the Nine-miles road crosses the railroad. I was about half a mile farther back, and the batteries of the enemy, on the left, were in his rear, but in front of the position where I was. As soon as General Hampton came up I directed him to take a by-road through the woods leading to the left and front; left orders for Hatton's brigade to come on by the main road, and moved forward to an open field upon the left hand side of the road. From this point I could, for the first time, see the relative positions of the batteries and the different brigades; I soon learned that General Whiting's brigade was returning to attack the batteries; that Pettigrew's brigade was also moving in that direction; that Hampton had come upon it and had already attacked, and that the three brigadier-generals were all apprised of each other's relative positions; and were acting in concert under Whiting's orders. The force of the enemy was not known, but it was confidently believed that we would soon capture or drive off the batteries and resume our march in support of Longstreet. The musketry fire increased, and after a short time, becoming impatient of the delay, I rode across the open field to the woods where the troops were engaged, and there learned from Colonel [afterward Lieutenant-General S. D.] Lee, [then] of the artillery, that General Hampton had driven the enemy some distance through the woods, but that they were being rapidly re-enforced and held a strong position, either fortified or offering natural shelter, and were fast extending beyond Hampton's left. The firing indicated that Whiting's brigade and Pettigrew's were fully occupied by the enemy in their immediate front. Hatton's brigade had in the meantime come up and was formed in the edge of the field near the Nine-miles road. Colonel [C. E.] Lightfoot's regiment, of Pettigrew's brigade, was in the field in reserve. On learning from Colonel Lee the condition of affairs in Hampton's front, I immediately ordered Hatton's brigade and Lightfoot's regiment to move forward. . . . I had not proceeded far into the wood before meeting with General Hampton. In a few words he communicated to me the state of affairs, and instructions were at once given for putting the brigade of General Hatton and Colonel Lightfoot's regiment in close action. At the time they were already under a deadly fire in a dense, entangled wood, struggling through the morass, covered with logs and thick bushes. . . . Coming up with the front line of troops already engaged . . . [Hatton's brigade] commenced firing, advancing upon the left to within fifteen or twenty yards of the line of fire of the enemy, which apparently came from the low bank of an old ditch, either a drain or the foundation of a fence. . . . Various attempts were made to charge the enemy, but without that concert of action almost absolutely necessary to success. . . . Our troops held their position close to the enemy's line until it was too dark to distinguish friend from foe. . . . The troops [on the line where I was] were withdrawn from the wooded swamp, immediately in contact with the enemy, and bivouacked in the open field. . . . After leaving the wood I heard for the first time that General Johnston had been severely wounded and compelled to leave the field. This unfortunate casualty placed me, as second in rank, in command of the Army of Northern Virginia."

General Hatton was killed just as his line reached Hampton's. A few minutes later General Hampton was severely wounded;

and I soon heard that General Pettigrew was wounded—perhaps mortally. In this condition of affairs in that wood, I sent word to General Whiting that I would remain at the front and take executive control of that part of the line, thus enabling him to give exclusive attention to his right. Just before dark the only troops of Magruder's command that were within reach—when I transmitted General Johnston's order for them to be brought up—arrived upon the field; but it was then too late to put them in action.

The losses in G. W. Smith's division, under Whiting, on the 31st of May, were 1,270. Of which 356 were in Whiting's brigade (under Law); 341 in Pettigrew's; 329 in Hampton's; and 244 in Hatton's. The fact that the Confederate losses were more than 1,200, whilst the Federal losses were less than 500, may be fairly attributed to the very effective fire of two Federal batteries in well-selected positions. The Confederates had no artillery on this field.

As General Keyes seems to attach some importance to his statement that, in this battle, "The Confederates" were "led on and cheered by" "the President of their Republic," it may be well to refer to what the latter says in regard to the part he played at Seven Pines. In "The Rise and Fall of the Confederate Government," Vol. II., p. 123, ex-President Davis states that: "When General Lee and I, riding down the Nine-miles road, reached the left of our line, we found the troops hotly engaged. Our men had driven the enemy from his advanced encampment, and he had fallen back behind an open field to the bank of the river, where, in a dense wood, was concealed an infantry line, with artillery in position. Soon after our arrival General Johnston, who had gone farther to the right, where the conflict was expected, and whither re-enforcement from the left was marching, was brought back severely wounded, and, as soon as an ambulance could be obtained, was removed from the field. Our troops on the left made vigorous assaults under most disadvantageous circumstances. They made several gallant attempts to carry the enemy's position, but were each time repulsed with heavy loss. After a personal reconnaissance on the left of the open in our front, I sent one, then another, and another courier to General Magruder, directing him to send a force down by the wooded path, just under the bluff, to attack the enemy in flank and reverse. Impatient of delay, I had started to see General Magruder, when I met the third courier, who said he had not found General Magruder, but had delivered the message to Brigadier-General Griffith, who was moving by the path designated to make the attack. On returning to the field, I found that the attack in front had ceased; it was, therefore, too late for a single brigade to effect anything against the large force of the enemy, and messengers were sent through the woods to direct General Griffith to go back."

It is more than two and a half miles from Fair Oaks Station to the river. "The enemy" fell back about half a mile from the station, and took position about two miles from the river, instead of on its bank, as asserted by ex-President Davis. He arrived on the field about the time General Johnston was wounded, and only commenced giving orders after the latter was removed from the field. It was then too late to bring up the nearest of Magruder's troops before dark, to say nothing of the additional time that would be required to send them "down by the wooded path, just under the bluff," "to the bank of the river," "to attack the enemy in flank and reverse." When the "third courier" met Griffith's brigade the latter was, no doubt, coming up under instructions I had transmitted from General Johnston, before the President and General Lee "reached the left of our line."

Whilst the ex-President says that he recalled Griffith's brigade, because he "found that the attack in front had ceased," and "it was, therefore, too late for a single brigade to effect anything against the large force of the enemy," he ignores the fact that the attack in front only ceased at dark; and would thus have it believed that his failure to accomplish important results, by the skilful use of one brigade, was caused by the untimely cessation of the attack in front.*

When I was informed that General Johnston had been wounded, I had not heard that President Davis was anywhere near the

---

* The ex-President *seems* not to have been aware that Sumner had advanced two miles from the river and was checked in his march to the assistance of Heintzelman and Keyes.   G. W. S.

field of operations. And I have reason to believe that of all the men in close action, that day, there were not ten who knew anything more of his presence than I did. Yet, stress is laid upon the claim that, on the 31st of May, "The Confederates" were "led on and cheered by" "the President of their Republic."

Within two or three minutes after hearing General Johnston had been wounded and taken from the field, I met President Davis. He was near the point where the Nine-miles road leaves the large wood which was the western border of the open field on the north side of that road. After saying that he supposed I knew the command of the army had devolved upon me, he asked me what were my plans. In reply I told him of General Johnston's intentions early that morning—referred to the misunderstanding which resulted in the unexpected transfer of Longstreet's division from the Nine-miles road to the Williamsburg road—the delay on the latter road, in commencing the attack—and to Longstreet's note received by Johnston about 4 P. M. I explained the nature of the contest in the woods where we had been closely engaged with Federal re-enforcements from the north side of the Chickahominy—and remarked that whilst we had not been able to drive them back, we had effectually barred their farther progress against Longstreet's left flank. The latter being the special purpose for which General Johnston had ordered my division, under Whiting, to move from the left wing of the army, near the Meadow Bridge road.

I then asked Mr. Davis, and those with him, if anything had been heard from the right wing, under Longstreet, later than the note just mentioned. Nothing farther had been heard. Mr. Davis again asked me what were my plans. I repeated what I had said in reference to General Johnston's intentions and expectations that morning—the delays—and the disappointment felt by General Johnston in the failure to strike an effective blow against the Federals, isolated near Seven Pines, early that morning, in time to regain position covering Richmond—before any attempt could be made against it, on the north side, by the large Federal force between New Bridge and Mechanicsville. But, that I could not determine, understandingly, what was best to be done until I knew what had occurred in the right wing.

Mr. Davis did not seem pleased with what I said. He makes no reference to any conference or conversation with me at that time; but, after stating that he sent messengers "through the woods to direct General Griffith to go back," he adds: "General Lee, at nightfall, gave instructions to General Smith, the senior officer on that part of the battle-field, and left with me to return to Richmond."

"General Smith" was then the senior officer of the Army of Northern Virginia, on that battle-field. General Lee gave him no instructions.

CHAPTER V.

THE FIGHTING, JUNE 1.

GENERAL SUMNER, in his official report, says: "On Sunday morning, June 1, at 6.30 o'clock, the enemy attacked us again in great fury, and this time the brunt of the action was borne by Richardson's division. This division was placed on Saturday night parallel with the railroad. . . . This was a most obstinate contest, continuing for four hours, in which our troops showed the greatest gallantry and determination and drove the enemy from the field."

Early on the morning of June 1, Sedgwick's division and Couch's cut-off forces were drawn up in line facing almost west; the left was a little north of the railroad, and a little east of Fair Oaks Station. Including Brady's, there were five batteries in position in Sedgwick's lines. General Burns, with four regiments, was detached to guard Sumner's communications.

General Israel B. Richardson, in his official report, says: "Finding I could not get my artillery through the deep mud, was forced to leave it, and followed General Sedgwick by another road. Getting on as fast as possible, we came up just after the firing of Generals Couch and Sedgwick had ceased, it being then dark [May 31]. On reporting to General Sumner, he ordered me to take position on the line of railroad and on the left of General Sedgwick, and to communicate with pickets of General Birney's brigade on my left. I placed the brigade of General French on the railroad, three regiments of General Howard in second line, three regiments of General Meagher in third line, and one of General Howard's (the Fifth New Hampshire) as the advance guard to the brigade of General French. . . . Sunday, June 1, at 3 o'clock in the morning, the division stood to arms. . . . Three [Confederate] regiments (Second and Fifth Texas and Second Mississippi) bivouacked within half musket shot of the New Hampshire regiment; and, [the latter] having retired before daylight, without noise or confusion, nothing was seen of the enemy until about 5 in the morning." Richardson's line faced nearly south.

Captain G. W. Hazzard, Chief of Artillery, Richardson's division, says: "Pettit's battery (B, First New York Artillery) . . . arrived on the battlefield of Fair Oaks about 4.30 o'clock Sunday morning and was placed by the division commander along the road which runs north from the railroad station. In this position this battery completely defended the only open ground by which the enemy could approach our position, namely, some cleared and level fields extending west and southwest from 900 to 1,500 yards, and bounded north and south by dense woods. [Pettit's battery faced nearly west, and was on the prolongation of Sedgwick's line]. Frank's battery (G, First New York Artillery) was placed 200 yards in rear [of] and at right angles to Pettit's battery, so as to drive back the enemy should he attempt to emerge from the woods which line the southern side of the railroad. My own battery (C, Fourth Artillery) was at first placed in reserve, but subsequently four pieces (12-pounders) were moved south to the railroad."

General French's line made a very acute angle with the railroad. He says: "At 5 o'clock A. M. I was authorized by General Richardson to move the length of three regiments to the left." The Sixty-sixth New York formed the right of French's line; next on its left came the Fifty-seventh New York; then the Fifty-third Pennsylvania; the Fifty-second New York formed the left of French's line.

General Howard says that, "at about 5 A. M." he "was directed to detach the Eighty-first Pennsylvania [of his brigade], Colonel Miller, to prolong the line of General French to the left. . . . On the execution of that order word was brought to me that the left of Colonel Miller extended in front and beyond the right of General Birney's brigade."

The Colonel commanding the Sixty-sixth New York, which formed the right of French's line, says that after making the flank movement to the left, above referred to, the left of his regiment rested on the railroad, " to which my line preserved an acute angle." French's line crossed the railroad at the left of the Sixty-sixth New York; his three other regiments and Howard's were in the prolongation of the line; but on the south side of the railroad—not far from it at any point.

General Birney, in his official report, says: "At 10 o'clock P. M. [May 31], I had my connection perfect with General French. I found the railroad embankment afforded natural rifle-pits, and posted my brigade behind them and bivouacked for the night, throwing out strong pickets. . . . My brigade, in the position to which it was assigned by me, did gallant service under Colonel Ward on the 1st of June, and protected partly by the railroad did great execution with little loss."

Colonel J. H. H. Ward, in his official report, says: "The Seventh Massachusetts [Devens's brigade, but then attached to Birney's] and Fourth Maine were stationed on the right and left of the railroad in the advanced field. . . . the Thirty-eighth New York, Fortieth New York and Third Maine in an oblique line across the woods and next field, connecting with General Kearney on the left."

It has already been stated that on the night of May 31, the brigades of Berry and Jameson, of Kearney's division, occupied the rifle-pits, of the third line of defence, on the north side of the Williamsburg road, extending nearly to the railroad. Colonel Ward adds: "Previous to the attack on Sunday morning [June 1] I was visited by yourself [Kearney's A. A. Adjutant General], with directions from General Kearney to hold my position and connect by skirmishers with the general at the rifle-pits, and that if attacked he would re-enforce me at once."

General Richardson, in his official report, after stating that "Nothing was seen of the enemy until about 5 in the morning," adds: "There is a large open field opposite my right front. About 1,000 yards across on the opposite side it is covered with timber, and at the time mentioned the enemy's pickets were deployed on the other side of this field and moving toward us. The head of a column of cavalry was also seen just in the edge of the woods; also some reconnoitering officers mounted. Captain Pettit's battery had just come up. . . . These pieces now opened their fire; . . . the skirmishers and cavalry broke and retired into the woods in rear. This no doubt was intended as the head of the real attack, to come down this open field, but no movement of the enemy in that direction, after our firing ceased, could be seen during the remainder of the day."

It will hereafter be plainly seen, from the Confederate accounts, that an attack, such as General Richardson describes, was not intended. There was no Confederate cavalry on that part of the field except couriers.

Continuing his report, General Richardson says : " At 6.30 o'clock A. M., . . . along the whole of our front line, the enemy opened a heavy rolling fire of musketry within fifty yards. Near our left two roads crossed the railroad, and up these the enemy moved his columns of attack, supported on his left by battalions deployed in line of battle in the woods, the whole line coming up to us at once and without skirmishers in advance, showing that they had a good and perfect knowledge of the ground."

Or—which will be seen hereafter—they had no knowledge of the ground.

General Richardson proceeds to say: " Our men returned the fire with vivacity and spirit, and it soon became the heaviest musketry firing that I had ever experienced, during an hour and a half, and the enemy interposed fresh regiments five different times, to allow their men to replenish their ammunition. The action had continued in this way about an hour. . . . I now ordered in General Howard to reinforce the first line. . . . Soon after this the whole line of the enemy fell back for the first time, unable to stand our fire, and for half an hour the firing ceased on both sides."

General W. H. French, in his official report, says : " A dense thicket and swamp . . . covered the approach of the enemy, who opened his fire at about fifty yards distance. Although this attack was bold and sudden the line never swerved. The fire was returned coolly and deliberately. The first attack was at once repulsed. After a few moments' pause the heads of several columns of the enemy threw themselves upon the intervals of the regiments on the right and left of the Fifty-second New York. For some time the most desperate efforts were made to break our line. . . . The left of the Fifty-third Pennsylvania, consisting of seven companies, led on by the gallant Colonel Brooke, repulsed them again and again. The dashing Colonel Frank, of the Fifty-second New York, after holding them in his front and finding them turning his left flank, threw back three companies to receive and repulse the attack. . . . I called on Brigadier-General Howard who, with the Sixty-first New York, was awaiting impatiently on the railroad in rear to pass my lines. This was done in the most regular manner."

General Howard, in his official report, says: " A staff officer of General French's brigade then brought word to me that the Fifty-second New York was falling back. I was directed to send the Sixty-first New York and Sixty-fourth New York to the support of General French. I took these regiments up the railroad, forming them in deployed line on this road in rear of General French's left [wing]. Here I learned that Colonel Miller, Eighty-first Pennsylvania, was killed at the first fire of the enemy, and that the right and left wings of that regiment had become separated, and that one wing was without a field officer. I directed Lieutenant Miles, my Aide-de-Camp, to collect the companies of that wing and to make the best disposition of it he could. . . . I immediately moved forward into the woods with the Sixty-first and Sixty-fourth New York."

When General French called upon General Howard to re-enforce the first line, the Eighty-first Pennsylvania, of Howard's brigade, which prolonged French's line to the left, had given way.

Lieutenant-Colonel C. F. Johnston, in his official report of the operations of that regiment, says: " On the first fire Colonel Miller fell, being killed instantly. The attack on our right was made by a superior force, representing that they were our friends. One regiment claimed to be Owens's regiment. Colonel Miller commanded the men to recover arms. In an instant a murderous fire was poured into the regiment at a distance of about 100 feet. The right wing fell back, returning the fire. Almost simultaneously the left flank was attacked by a large force, led by a man bearing a white flag. They [the left wing] fell back. . . . The right wing . . . was formed by their officers in an open field on the north of the railroad. A portion of the left wing, being separated from the regiment, took up a position on the railroad, and continued firing until all their ammunition was expended. The regiment being formed, I took up a position on the edge of the woods, supporting the party on the railroad. I reported to headquarters for orders, and was ordered by General Sumner to remain in the position I then held until further orders." This regiment remained in that position until the fighting was over.

Reference will now be made to the movements in other portions of the Federal lines, caused by the driving back of the Eighty-first Pennsylvania, and the determined attack upon the left wing of French's brigade. Meagher's brigade was ordered into the gap on French's left; Pettit's battery was ordered from the right of Richardson's line to the left, and four guns of Hazzard's battery were brought to the front. Captain Hazzard says: "Ten horses were required to move our guns from one part of the field to another, and our wheel-traces and prolonges snapped like pack-threads." Burns's brigade—which was protecting the communications—was ordered back to Richardson's assistance.

So far Birney's brigade had not taken an active part in the main fighting. Colonel Ward, commanding this brigade, says: "A new fire was opened in the woods to my right and diagonally to my front. I immediately changed front to face the woods from where the fire emanated, and as the enemy advanced and their fire increased, I gave the order to fire and immediately thereafter to charge. This movement was most brilliantly performed, driving the enemy before them. This brilliant feat was accomplished by the Third Maine, Thirty-eighth and Fortieth New York. The enemy now retreating to the opening beyond, were met by a destructive flank fire from the Fourth Maine and Seventh Massachusetts, stationed on the railroad. The rout was complete."

Major W. H. Baird, commanding the Thirty-eighth New York, says: This regiment "was formed in line of battle at daybreak, my right resting near the railroad and connecting on the left with the right of the Third Maine. . . . We remained under arms until 8 o'clock A. M. In the meantime I had detached . . . two companies . . . to deploy and act as

skirmishers. . . . They skirmished back in good order, keeping the enemy in check until within less than 100 yards of our front. I then repeated Colonel Ward's order to 'Fire, charge and give them the bayonet'. . . . After delivering our fire we charged through the woods, driving the enemy before us at every point, and at last routed him completely. . . .
Fearing I should receive the fire of the Fourth Maine, which was stationed on the railroad at right angles with our own front, pouring a murderous fire on the enemy's left flank, I ordered a halt . . . and fell back to assume the same position occupied before the action."

Colonel H. G. Staples, of the Third Maine, says: " By your [Colonel Ward's] order we charged over the fence, and I am pleased to say that the command was gallantly executed, the regiment, cheering continually, rushed on the enemy with such impetuosity that they broke and fled at the first onset. We pursued them for a mile through woods and swamps, they endeavoring in vain to check us during their retreat by a rapid fire. When we crossed the run we met their reserve in large numbers on the top of an eminence; our brave boys, still advancing, threw themselves upon the ground half way up the hill and fired upon them steadily, the rebels returning our fire with terrible effect at this point, and most of our casualties took place here. After silencing their fire, by your order we retired and formed a line with the rest of the brigade."

Lieutenant-Colonel T. W. Egan, commanding the Fortieth New York, says: " About 8 o'clock in the morning, . . . on an order from Colonel J. H. H. Ward, who was commanding the brigade, I wheeled the battalion to the right, in order to face the enemy, and under a galling fire charged over the fence into the woods, our men at the same time delivering a vigorous fire upon the rebels."

It will hereafter be made clear that the Confederates encountered later, by the Fortieth New York, were not at any time near Richardson's line. The same may be said in reference to the Confederates who were met by Hooker's troops, who advanced about the time that Birney's brigade did. This branch of the subject will be taken up after finishing the account of operations in Richardson's front.

The Confederates who attacked the left wing of French's brigade and broke through the Eighty-first Pennsylvania, were subjected to a strong flank fire from the Fourth Maine and the Seventh Massachusetts. Colonel E. Walker, of the Fourth Maine, after describing the movements of four companies of his regiment under Captain Pitcher, that were strongly posted, well to the front, as skirmishers, to check and delay the enemy, known to be advancing through the woods, says: "I found the enemy had attacked and driven in the [Eighty-first] Pennsylvania, of General Howard's brigade, on the right and in front of Captain Pitcher's command. . . . The enemy soon appeared in large force at the edge of the woods, but were repulsed and held in check by these four companies until the [Thirty-eighth] New York formed in their rear; . . . he [Pitcher] withdrew to the same line, took position on the left of the other regiment, and continued his fire. While the enemy were engaged by them at short range on the left they [the enemy] also suffered severely from the raking fire of the remainder of the regiment at longer distance. They must have sustained great loss, too, from the cross-fire of the whole while retiring through the slashing before the other regiments of this [Birney's] brigade."

These events were transpiring beyond Richardson's left, about the time General Howard passed two of his regiments to the front of French's left wing, and took up the fighting on that part of the field. Extracts will now be given from the official report of the commander of each of these two regiments of Howard's brigade.

Colonel F. C. Barlow, Sixty-first New York, says, "Immediately on our left was the Sixty-fourth New York. . . . The firing in the woods in our front was very brisk, and we were immediately ordered by the General commanding the brigade to advance. We advanced in a woods of tall trees, thickly interspersed with an undergrowth of young oaks, which rendered it impossible for us to see to any great distance before us; the ground in some places was muddy and marshy. After advancing some 150 yards we came upon the Fifty-third Pennsylvania, Colonel Brooke, formed in line and briskly engaging the enemy. I requested Colonel Brooke to cease firing that we might pass in front of and relieve him; this was done, and we at once advanced upon the enemy, who were drawn up in line before us, and who kept up a heavy firing; after advancing some twenty-five yards beyond Colonel Brook's regiment I halted the regiment and fired one or two rounds; the enemy fell back firing, out of sight among the thick undergrowth; not willing to deliver our fire until we could see those opposed to us, I ordered the regiment to cease firing. . . . We then moved forward in excellent order some 180 yards, meeting with a heavy fire, but not seeing the enemy with sufficient distinctness to warrant, in my opinion, our halting and renewing the fire. On arriving upon the crest of a hill within some twenty yards of the road running parallel to the railroad . . . the battalion was halted, the enemy being plainly in sight by the roadside, and at once opened fire, receiving a very heavy one in return; this continued considerable time, and it was there that our principal loss occurred. We drove the enemy back, and he ceased firing. . . . I considered it unwise to advance farther, as there were no regiments on our flanks and we were considerably in advance of the line in our rear. . . . Finding that our flanks were not supported, I sent to ask Colonel Brooke to bring up his regiment upon our line, which he did; scarcely any firing was done after his arrival. . . . With orders from the General commanding the division for us to retire, we marched off in perfect order by the road leading to our right and returned to the field whence we started. We were not again engaged. . . . Our wounded, who were left on the ground, state that the position was occupied by the enemy immediately after we left it. . . . This regiment took some ten prisoners. . . . From these prisoners and from some of our wounded I learned that the force opposed to us was the Third Alabama . . . supported by the Twelfth and Forty-first Virginia."

These three regiments constituted Mahone's brigade of Huger's division, which attacked French's left wing. But they formed no part of the Confederate force from whose front Howard's regiments were withdrawn.

Colonel T. J. Parker, of the Sixty-fourth New York, on the left of the Sixty-third—in Howard's movement to the front of

French's left wing—says: "On advancing through a thick woods on the south side of the railroad under a shower of balls from the enemy, General O. O. Howard and his Aide, C. H. Howard, were both severely wounded near our line. On arriving within about fifty yards of the enemy's line we opened fire upon them. They fought desperately, being soon re-enforced, and the battle raged about two hours, both lines holding their position. We then charged bayonet on them, they falling back in disorder, leaving their dead and wounded on the field. I then received orders to reform the line in rear of General Meagher's brigade."

The following extracts from the official report of Colonel E. E. Cross, of the Fifth New Hampshire, show that the "bayonet charge" described by Colonel Parker was not so effective as might be inferred from his words. Colonel Cross says: "I received notice that Brigadier-General Howard was severely wounded, and the command of the first brigade devolved upon me. Finding that the three other regiments of the brigade had been some time in action and severely handled, I directed that they should move out of the woods, and reform in rear of Meagher's brigade, while I advanced my regiment to occupy the ground. We moved forward in line of battle through a thick woods, and about 300 yards from the railroad track encountered the rebel line of battle, and a fierce fire commenced on both sides. Twice my line advanced in the most gallant style, and each time the enemy fell back. The fire was now very close and deadly, the opposing lines being several times not over thirty yards apart. When about ordering another charge I was struck by a rifle-ball in the thigh and disabled. Lieutenant-Colonel Langley then took command of the regiment, and the rebels endeavoring to flank us, he brought off the regiment in excellent order, carrying most of our wounded."

French's right was not attacked. When the action was virtually over that wing advanced into the woods—came across two Confederate regiments, that were, by mistake, firing into each other; and one of the latter regiments, which had just gone into the woods, fell back in confusion, more afraid of friends than of foes. This accidental *fiasco* has been very much magnified. In certain quarters it has been accepted as convincing proof that the Federals gained an "overwhelming victory." The Sixty-sixth New York, which, it is claimed, effected these results by "a bayonet charge," lost, that day, one enlisted man killed and five enlisted men wounded! During this advance into the woods French's right wing did not touch the Confederate position—in front of his left wing—about 300 yards south of the railroad.

From the Federal accounts it is clear that a determined, persistent and staggering blow was made against the left of Richardson's front line; the Confederates who made that attack were finally repulsed by fresh troops from Richardson's second line, and by Birney's brigade of Kearney's division. One regiment of the latter, however, and three regiments of Howard's brigade, ran against a Confederate force which had not attacked Richardson. That force successfully resisted these four regiments. General Richardson states that the number of his "division engaged was about 7,000." The official records show that his aggregate losses were 838, of which number 557 were in Howard's brigade.

The aggregate losses in Birney's brigade were 207. But, one regiment of the latter brigade, in its advance, passed south of the Confederate position above referred to, and ran against another Confederate force in the vicinity of the Williamsburg road. That regiment was the Fortieth New York, commanded by Lieutenant-Colonel Egan, whose official report has already been partly quoted. Continuing his report, he says: "I then ordered my men to charge bayonets, and in an instant they were advancing at double-quick, which the enemy perceiving, and not relishing the idea of cold steel, turned and fled. We continued driving them to the front and when near the edge of the woods we received a heavy fire from the front and left. Here many of our men fell, notwithstanding which not one faltered, but with tremendous cheers continued to advance, driving the enemy entirely from the woods and scattering them in all directions, notwithstanding they made a desperate resistance."

General Hooker, in his official report, says: "Apparently the enemy were actively engaged with the troops of Sumner's corps, and in making for the heaviest fire my object was to attack in rear and destroy him. On the route, and near by the enemy, I passed on my right a brigade of Kearney's division, under Colonel Ward. . . . As there was delay, orders were given Colonel Ward to support my command; . . . his brigade was brought into action on the right of the New Jersey regiments [which formed the right of Hooker's line; Sickles's brigade being on the left]. From the beginning of the action our advance on the rebels along the whole line was slow, but I could feel that it was positive and unyielding. Our lines were well preserved, the fire brisk and unerring, and our troops reliant—all the omens of success. After an interchange of musketry of this character for more than an hour, directions were given to advance with the bayonet, when the enemy were thrown into wild confusion, throwing away their arms, hats and coats and broke through the forest in the direction of Richmond. At this moment chivalry and rebellion presented a deplorable picture. Pursuit was hopeless. This being ended, and no other fire heard on any part of the field, the troops were ordered to return to their respective camps. The engagement lasted upwards of two hours, and almost all our loss occurred prior to the bayonet charge. The movements of the rebels on Sunday indicate that their purpose was to finish the business they had commenced on Saturday. The column attacked and routed were attempting to force their way over the belt of land lying between the Williamsburg Old Stage road and the railroad, in the direction of our depots in rear." *

The losses in the two New Jersey regiments were 79; in the five regiments of Sickles's brigade, 74. The reports of subordinate commanders show that Sickles's brigade remained on the ground from which the Confederates retired. Aggregate losses in Hooker's division, 153.

It will presently be seen that the Confederates opposed to Hooker were withdrawn in compliance with a positive written order from General D. H. Hill. The so-called "bayonet charge"

---

* In his official report General Hooker mentions that his "Chief of Artillery attempted to follow with his batteries, but was prevented by the miry condition of the fields through which we were compelled to pass." G. W. S.

did not drive them back. The "column" which Hooker claims to have routed was not attempting "to force its way in the direction of" the Federal "depots in rear."

Confederate Accounts.—In his official report, already quoted, General Wilcox continues: "My line remained as formed [in the vicinity of Casey's redoubt just before night, May 31,] till 10 P. M., and was then ordered, together with Pryor's brigade, near a mile to the front on the road to relieve [R. H.] Anderson's brigade. . . . Soon after daylight, the following morning, a few musketry shots were heard, revealing the fact that the enemy were in our front and rear. Dispositions were promptly made for a renewal of the fight. The position held by my troops was near a mile in advance of the captured batteries and rifle-pits [Casey's headquarters]. . . . The Nineteenth Mississippi had been ordered to report to General [R. H.] Anderson the previous evening, and had been thrown forward a few hundred yards farther on the road. . . . Pryor's brigade had bivouacked a few hundred yards in rear of mine, but was moved near after daylight, but not until a few shots had been exchanged between the pickets. The field in which my brigade bivouacked was inclosed by a heavy forest, filled with a thick entangled undergrowth of bushes and branches. The ground [was] low and in many places boggy and covered with water. Having no knowledge of the ground or of the position and strength of the enemy, I did not feel justified in making an advance, but made such disposition of my troops as to be prepared to meet the enemy in any direction he might appear, awaiting orders in the meantime."

General Wilcox states in detail the location of every regiment in the two brigades ; gives a description of the initial firing, and adds : "The men were eager for the fight, and everything seemed to indicate a success as full and complete as the day previous. The Nineteenth Mississippi had already repulsed the enemy in its front, the other troops were doing well, and the engagement, now raging furiously, was going on as well as could be desired ; but just at this time an order in writing was sent to me to withdraw my command, which was instantly done, my brigade retiring by the right flank and keeping in the woods. Pryor's brigade following [falling?] back directly across the open field in rear, being pursued by the enemy to the field and experiencing some loss as it entered it. The enemy did not cross the field and soon ceased firing. The two brigades were now moved back to near the field in which were the captured batteries and rifle-pits, referred to above, formed in line and facing to the north side of the road."

In a postscript General Wilcox says: " The order given me to retire my command on the second morning was given in writing by D. H. Hill, and for the reason, as he stated in his note, that Mahone's men had acted badly." No report seems to have been made by General Pryor or any of his regimental commanders. General Wilcox says: " Pryor's brigade was not engaged on the 31st but acted well on the second day, and yielded reluctantly to the order to withdraw." No statement of the losses in this brigade is found.

The losses in Wilcox's brigade in both days are stated by him to have been 110. Of that number he says 66 were killed and wounded in the only three companies of his brigade that were put in action the first day. These three companies accomplished in a few minutes the work to which they were assigned. The conduct of those companies in action, May 31, may be taken as an indication of the reception Hooker would have met with on the 1st of June, if the brigades of Wilcox and Pryor had not been withdrawn in compliance with a peremptory order given by D. H. Hill.

In reference to the operations of Mahone's brigade, in this action, no official report is found from any one connected with that brigade. But the following extracts from correspondence throw light upon the subject. In a letter dated October 13, 1862, addressed to Captain Benjamin Huger, General Mahone says: "About 1 o'clock that night [he means 1 A. M. June 1] I received an order from General Huger directing me to move at daylight for the battle-field of ' Seven Pines ' where I would report to Major-General D. H. Hill. In accordance with this order the brigade moved and reported to General Hill about 7 A. M., June 1, or perhaps earlier, at the same time General Pickett's brigade reported upon the field. The brigade [Mahone's] was in a few moments thereafter, thrown into action, a report upon which General Huger has." No trace of that report is found.

In a letter dated December 14, 1885, addressed to me, General Mahone says that at the time of the battle of Seven Pines two regiments of his brigade "had been temporarily detached leaving with him only the Twelfth and Forty-first Virginia and the Third Alabama Regiments." After stating that his brigade relieved that of General Rodes, on the Charles City road, May 31; he adds, "Late that night I received orders to move the next morning at daylight to the battle-field of Seven Pines, and there report to General D. H. Hill. I moved the brigade . . . (starting before day) directly and speedily as possible to Seven Pines, and forming my brigade in line, just in rear or south of the works from which the enemy had been driven, on the right hand or south side of the main road, and quite opposite General Casey's headquarters tent, now occupied by General D. H. Hill. I reported in person to General Hill at this tent. At the moment I was reporting to General Hill some person rode up and excitedly stated to him that the enemy were in the wood on the north side of the road and were moving down upon his then headquarters. General Hill said: 'General Mahone take your brigade *in there*,' referring to the wood in which the enemy were said to be, and moving as just stated. Immediately I put my brigade in motion, by column of companies for the wood, and I had given the order 'right and forward into line,' which would have brought the three regiments facing the enemy, when I discovered that my rear regiment, the Twelfth Virginia, had been detached and sent off in another direction by General Hill. . . . The Forty-first Virginia and the Third Alabama were quickly brought into line . . . and without halting rushed forward into the woods . . . until we reached the re-enforced line of the enemy. . . . Meanwhile the Forty-first Virginia and Third Alabama had become separated in the dense wood. Lomax, Colonel of the Third Alabama had been killed, and the regiment had fallen into some confusion. At this juncture the Twelfth Virginia had reached me, and while under a pressing fire from the enemy, by some misunderstanding fell back, when I was about to order it to charge. In this condition of things I reformed my brigade on the line of the main road. . . . There was nothing more of consequence done that day."

In a letter to me dated December 25, 1885, General Mahone says: The "second attack" described by General Richardson, was " doubtless the charge of the Third Alabama and the Forty-first Virginia. . . . The impetus of the charge of the Third Alabama, a splendid regiment, I am satisfied must have severely shocked and disordered his [Richardson's] line; and if there had been any intelligent understanding of the position of the enemy, and instructions as to what we were to do, it can be seen now how easy a destructive blow might have been given; but, 'Take your brigade in there;' to one just reaching the field, can scarcely be taken as evidence that the commanding officer knew what he was about." "I also remember to have seen Colonel Tomlin's regiment of Armistead's brigade immediately following the charge of the Third Alabama. It came up in good order and halted . . . between the Third Alabama and Forty-first Virginia. After receiving a fire from the enemy (all woods) Colonel Tomlin's regiment suddenly retired. . . . It was just after this that the Twelfth Virginia, which had been detached by General Hill, came up. . . . Meanwhile the Third Alabama had advanced far into the wood to the north. . . . And hotly engaged the enemy—and doubtless being overlapped and greatly outnumbered, and, having lost its Colonel, was broken and remarched to the open field and reformed . . . on the most advantageous line."

On the 6th of January, 1886, General Mahone wrote me: "I am quite certain that Armistead's brigade was on my immediate right. . . . There was no fighting which would indicate an attack by either side before my two regiments went in as described in previous letters and none on my left during the engagement that followed. Armistead's brigade and mine must have struck the enemy about the same time. I cannot give you, I am sorry to say, reliable estimate of my loss."

In a letter to me, March 9, 1886, Governor W. E. Cameron, who was Adjutant of the Twelfth Virginia, at Seven Pines, corroborates in the main what is said above by General Mahone, and adds: the losses in the Twelfth Virginia were "9 killed, 31 wounded, 1 officer and 11 men unaccounted for, a total of 52. The Forty-first [Virginia], 11 killed, 44 wounded," "1 officer and 56 men" "missing." "It was discovered afterward that a large proportion of the men of both regiments, reported missing or unaccounted for, had been killed or wounded, but I am only able to get now the reports made on the field through the Medical and Adjutant-General Departments."

On the 30th of March, 1886, Robert M. Sands, Captain, Mobile Cadets, Company A, Third Alabama Infantry, A. N. V., in a letter addressed to me, says:

"In answer to your inquiry regarding the loss of the Third Alabama at Seven Pines, I, having just counted *by names*, from a detailed report, make it as follows: killed 38, wounded 123, missing 14, total 175, including our Colonel, Lomax, and his Adjutant."

The total losses in the three regiments of Mahone's brigade in this action are thus shown to have been 338. One of Mahone's regiments was detached at Chafin's Bluff and one at Gordonsville.

In his official report Colonel H. B. Tomlin, of the Fifty-third Virginia, Armistead's brigade, says: that, upon reaching the Williamsburg road from the Charles City road, late in the afternoon, May 31, the regiment "was ordered by Major-General Longstreet to remain as a reserve with him until further orders. It was then detached from General Armistead's brigade. Early next morning I dispatched Major G. M. Waddill to report the above fact to General Armistead, to ascertain the position he occupied, and to report that I would join him with my regiment as soon as relieved. . . . Upon reaching Seven Pines [he means Casey's redoubt and rifle-pits], Major G. M. Waddill indicated the direction in which General Armistead had gone, and informed me that his Adjutant had sent me instructions to deploy on the left of the Ninth Virginia, then not in sight, and saying it had entered the woods near a given point. Just before this point was reached the order was given to form column by companies and then forward into line of battle. And though this movement was executed in double-quick time, before it was executed we received a heavy cross-fire from the right and left, which was immediately returned. Seeing no enemy, and having received no other order than the one above recited, I ordered the men to lie down. Discovering troops coming toward our right wing with white bands on their hats [I] ordered mine not to fire, that they were friends; but the fire continuing [ed] down the whole line, yet too high to do much injury. Some one, without authority, in the right wing gave the command to retreat, which was passed down the whole line by the Captains, and the men fell back in great disorder into the field on which they had just emerged; reformed, and, with every company in proper position in line of battle, double-quicked it back into the woods, and shortly after crossing the road came up with the Forty-first Virginia, marching directly toward us. From this direction we received a constant fire, which we returned until some of our officers, recognizing some of the officers of the Forty-first Virginia (Major G. M. Waddill, who was upon the left wing, while I was at that time upon the right), commanded them to march in retreat. At this time my horse was killed, and not hearing the command nor knowing the cause [I] attempted to rally the men; . . . friends and enemies were so indiscriminately mixed up together that it was most advisable to return to the open field. We returned slowly to the field, apprehending more danger from friends than the enemy. We again reformed and reported for duty to Major-General Hill."

This regiment was then posted in the open space around Casey's earthworks, and finally " joined General Armistead's brigade (late in the afternoon), which we met with for the first time during the day, placed on the outer post nearest the enemy." Colonel Tomlin reports 1 killed, 18 wounded and 3 missing. Total losses, 22.

No other official report from any one connected with Armistead's brigade is found among the records. By correspondence and inquiry I have not been able to obtain any material facts in reference to this brigade, that day, other than those already stated.

There is, however, very distinct reference made to Armistead's brigade in the official report of Brigadier-General George E. Pickett, who says that "about 9 P. M.," May 31, he received orders from General Longstreet to march his brigade at daylight [June 1] and report to Major-General D. H. Hill, at or near Seven Pines. Pickett adds: "[I] found General Hill at General Casey's late headquarters, just in rear of enemy's redoubt—'The Redoubt.' My brigade had marched some 400 yards in advance of this point when it was there halted. General Hill directed me to ride over to the railroad and communicate with Brigadier-General Hood, whose right was resting on that road. I asked General Hill of the whereabouts of the enemy. He said they were some distance in advance—in fact, I had no definite idea where, as I saw no one, and had not had time to examine the nature of [the] ground or the position. With two of my staff officers . . . I proceeded through the undergrowth and thickets towards the railroad some 400 yards, when I was met by a party of the Louisiania Zouaves (who had evidently been on a plundering expedition) rushing past me at a most headlong speed. One fellow, riding a mule with a halter, I seized on and detained for explanation. He said the enemy were within a few yards of us, and entreated me to let him save himself. I immediately rode back with him at a gallop, and as briefly as possible informed General Hill of the circumstances. He ordered me to attack, and I supposed [the] same order was given to other brigade commanders. I rejoined my brigade at once, and by a change of front forward put it in line of battle nearly perpendicular to the railroad and advanced. Armistead on my left, and Pryor and Wilcox (the latter I did not see, but heard he was there) on my right, struck the enemy within a short distance (who opened heavily on us), drove him through an abatis, over a crossroad leading to railroad, and was advancing over a second abatis when I had discovered Armistead's brigade had broken and were leaving the field pell-mell. At this moment I was on foot and half-way across the abatis, the men moving on beautifully and carrying everything before them. I could scarcely credit my own eyes in witnessing this misfortune on my left. I immediately rode to that part of [the] field, found nothing between me and [the] railroad except the gallant Armistead himself, with a regimental color and some thirty persons, mostly officers, with him. I saw our danger at once and dispatched a courier to General Hill, asking for more troops to cover the vacuum. Receiving no reply, and the enemy pressing forward in force, brigade after brigade,* and threatening my left flank, I threw back the left wing of the Nineteenth Virginia, the left regiment, so as to oppose a front to them, dispatched a staff officer to General Hill with [a] request for troops; and after a while sent a second dispatch, similarly worded. As a matter of course, from having been the attacking party, I now had to act on the defensive. Fortunately the enemy seemed determined on attacking and carrying my front and driving me out of the abatis, which our men succeeded in preventing, though with considerable loss."

When Pickett formed his brigade "in line of battle nearly perpendicular to the railroad," and advanced, the direction of his movement was toward the east, nearly parallel to Richardson's front. There is reason to believe that such opposition as Pickett met with—whilst his troops were "moving on beautifully," through abatis, etc., parallel to and 300 or 400 yards south of the railroad—was from the strong skirmish lines thrown well to their front, on the south side of the railroad, by regiments of Birney's brigade, for the purpose of holding the Confederate advance in check long enough to enable Kearney to come, from the trenches in the third line of defense, to Birney's assistance. Before Pickett found himself constrained to act on the defensive, in the abatis, his brigade had met with no material opposition. From his description of all his operations it is clear that his brigade never touched Richardson's line. While he was "moving on beautifully;" against Federal regimental grand-guards and skirmishers; he seems to have been serenely unconscious that a few hundred yards on his left, in the dense and tangled wood, other Confederate troops had struck the main line of the enemy near the railroad.

He adds: "Hearing nothing from General Hill, I rode as rapidly as possible to him, and explained as laconically [as I could] the position of affairs. He asked me if I could not withdraw my

---

* Federal accounts already quoted show that Pickett's position was attacked by four regiments in all.

brigade. I said yes, but did not wish to do so; that I would leave all my wounded, lose many more men, and that the enemy would pour down on the disorganized mass, as he himself termed the troops about him. He then sent two regiments of Colston's brigade, which my Assistant Adjutant-General, Captain Pickett, put in position on my left, and asked me to take Mahone's brigade and put it on my right, which was done. . . . A brigade debouched from the piece of woods in my front and moved steadily toward my left flank. They came up to within about range, when their commander, seeing his men about to commence firing, stopped them (and) called out, 'What troops are these?' Some of our men shouted 'Virginians.' He then cried out, 'don't fire, they'll surrender; we'll capture all these d——d Virginians.' Scarcely were the words uttered when the Nineteenth and left of the Eighteenth rose up in the abatis and fired a withering volley into them, killing * their commanding officer and literally mowing down their ranks. Just then Colston's regiments came up on the left and Mahone's on the right. The enemy retreated to their bushy cover and their fire immediately slackened. No other attempt was made by them to advance, and about 1 P. M., I judge, by General Hill's order, I withdrew the whole of our front line, Pryor and Wilcox, and some other troops I do not remember, being in position some 400 yards in our rear. We withdrew in perfect order, not a gun was fired at us, and bringing off all our wounded. This was the conclusion of the battle of Seven Pines."

Whilst Pickett was thus appealing for help in order to enable him to prevent the enemy from pouring down on the disorganized mass, as he says (D. H. Hill) himself " termed the troops around him "—the latter was endeavoring to concentrate the whole thirteen brigades of the right wing " around the captured works, in the hope that the Yankees would attempt to retake them." The " disorganized mass," Pickett speaks of, contained the five brigades that had done all the bloody fighting under Hill on the previous day—in addition to two brigades of Longstreet's division and one brigade of Huger's division that were not in close

---

* But see the report of the Colonel of the Fifth New Hampshire.

action either day—besides the two brigades under Wilcox that had been withdrawn, from their position east of Seven Pines, by D. H. Hill's order.

General Pickett states that his brigade consisted of four regiments; "aggregate, 1,700. Loss, 350 killed and wounded; no prisoners."

CHAPTER VI.

LONGSTREET IN THE FIELD, JUNE 1.—D. H. HILL'S OFFICIAL REPORT.—WITHDRAWAL OF THE CONFEDERATES FROM THE CAPTURED WORKS, JUNE 2.

Just after President Davis left the front, about dark, May 31, I sent for General Longstreet to come as soon as possible to the headquarters on the Nine-miles road near Old Tavern. I then directed General Whiting to care for the wounded and dead of the division he commanded, assign proper officers to take charge of the three brigades that had lost their regular commanders, see that the vacant places among the field and company officers were properly filled, and place the division in position confronting the enemy; his own brigade and Hood's in first line, the three other brigades within close supporting distance.

A few minutes later, General J. E. B. Stuart, the commander of the cavalry of Johnston's army, reached me and reported that the Federals had made no advance on the Charles City road; that our troops had captured the works at Seven Pines (Couch's line) some time before sunset, and had advanced beyond that point; he did not know to what distance, or in what numbers. He had good guides with him, and offered to go in person to General Longstreet, and have him piloted to my headquarters.

I then left the front and returned to the house from which General Johnston so hurriedly moved forward "against the right flank of Longstreet's adversaries," immediately after he received the note, previously referred to, complaining of his "slowness." When I returned from the front I knew nothing more, in regard to the operations of the right wing, than the information contained in that note, and the report made to me by General Stuart. The latter information indicated that Longstreet's three divisions, unaided by the division Johnston pressed forward to his assistance, had succeeded in driving the enemy from their second line.

The Federal re-enforcements encountered by the division under Whiting were in large numbers. How many more might be sent over the river during the night, or early next morning, we had no means of estimating. So far from its being then known to us that the bridges had been swept away,* and the Chickahominy rendered impassable, *we had good reason to believe the contrary.*

After my arrival at the headquarters, about 9 p. m., I received the following from General McLaws, who commanded a division of four brigades, forming a part of the centre of the army under General Magruder. McLaws wrote: "I am at the position opposite the New Bridge. The Colonel in command informs me that there is a heavy force opposite this point, and that this evening the pickets reported that the enemy had been throwing heavy objects in the river. As pontoon boats have been seen there, it is supposed they are making a pontoon bridge. The force to guard this point is two regiments. . . . If this position is forced, your command will be in great danger, as you are aware."

On receipt of the foregoing, I requested General McLaws to let me know the exact position of his troops. In his reply, dated 11 p. m., May 31, he says: "The positions of the troops are as follows: General Cobb, five regiments, from the Mechanicsville road to General Harvey's place; General Kershaw from General Harvey's to Barker's; Generals Griffith and Semmes from General Kershaw's right to New Bridge, and on the line down New Bridge road and across the country to the railroad."

The rest of Magruder's command—D. R. Jones's division, two brigades—were in position on the Meadow Bridge road and the Mechanicsville road.

General A. P. Hill, temporarily commanding the left wing in the vicinity of Meadow Bridge, reported that all had been quiet, in his front, during the day, but the enemy's batteries at Mechanicsville had been firing heavily without inflicting any material damage. A short time before midnight I received a note from General Stuart stating that, at 10.30 p. m., he had failed to find

---

* Both of Sumner's bridges were washed away soon after his corps had crossed.

General Longstreet. At that time I was under the distinct impression that there was a gap, nearly a mile in extent, between Whiting's right and Longstreet's left. Whiting's left was in the air in the direction of New Bridge.

At 12.40 A. M., June 1, no further information had been received in regard to the operations of the right wing. I had several hours previously heard from all other portions of the army. I then wrote to General Longstreet asking the position of his command, the condition of his men, and requesting his views in regard to future operations in his front. After that note was written, one of my staff officers, who had been sent to Longstreet, just after dark, came in, bringing General Longstreet with him. The note had not been received. He reported that only a portion of his own division had been seriously engaged—Huger's division had not been engaged at all—the principal fighting had been done by D. H. Hill's division—the enemy's second line of works had been carried late in the afternoon—their forces pressed back about one mile—the fighting continued until dark—and his three divisions were all at last well up to the front.

Longstreet showed no disposition to renew the attack with the right wing. When I indicated to him that this must be done, he insisted that the attack had better be made by the division under Whiting—supported by the right wing. I then gave him positive orders to send one brigade to the Nine-miles road, and attack with the remainder of the right wing as soon after daybreak as possible; and fight towards the north instead of attempting to force his way any further toward Bottom's Bridge. He was assured that when the attack I ordered him to make was fully developed, it should be supported by the division under Whiting; and, if necessary, by the forces then guarding the crossings of the Chickahominy.

Between 2 and 3 A. M. he left me for the purpose, as I had reason to believe, of carrying into effect the orders he had received. I never doubted that this was his intention until I saw General D. H. Hill's official report, in the Records recently published by the United States War Department.

After Longstreet left me, I notified Whiting, Magruder, and A. P. Hill, that the attack would be renewed by the right wing very soon after daylight, and directed them to be ready to make any movement that might be ordered. I then wrote to General Lee, who was stationed in Richmond, and had, under President Davis, general charge of all Confederate military operations, telling him I had determined to renew the attack with the right wing, and asking him for all the assistance he could give. The following is a copy of General Lee's reply:

* "RICHMOND,
1st June, '62, 5 A. M.

General:

"Your letter of this morning just received. Ripley will be ordered and such forces from General Holmes as can be got up will be sent. Your movements are judicious and determination to strike the enemy right. Try and ascertain his position and how he can best be hit. I will send such engineers as I can raise. But with Stevens, Whiting, Alexander, etc., what can I give you like them. You are right in calling upon me for what you want. I wish I could do more. It will be a glorious thing if you can gain a complete victory. Our success on the whole yesterday was good, but not complete.

"Truly,
"R. E. LEE,
"General.

"General G. W. SMITH,
"Commander Army of Northern Virginia."

Magruder was directed to place Cobb's and Kershaw's brigades nearer to New Bridge, and hold them in readiness to replace the troops at that point, and along the New Bridge road, so the latter could promptly re-enforce Whiting, when the latter should advance to co-operate in the attack Longstreet was ordered to make. A. P. Hill was instructed to hold his division ready to march to the right.

In my official report it is stated that:

"Between 2 and 3 o'clock in the morning of June 1, I had a conference with General Longstreet, and learning that he had ordered General Huger's division, which had not been engaged upon

---

* A *fac-simile* of this note is given on page 179.

May 31, to move from the Charles City to the Williamsburg stage road, one of the brigades of this division was directed to take position as soon as practicable upon the Nine-miles road; and, together with that of General Ripley [then expected to arrive], form a reserve for my division, which General Whiting commanded. The troops of the left wing [under A. P. Hill] and of the centre [under Magruder] remained substantially in the positions occupied the previous day, protecting our rear and the City of Richmond from any movement of the enemy across the Chickahominy at or above New Bridge. General Longstreet was directed to push his successes of the previous day as far as practicable, pivoting his movement upon the position of General Whiting on his left. The latter was directed to make a diversion in favor of General Longstreet's real attack; and, if pressed by the enemy, hold at all hazards the fork, or junction, of the New Bridge and Nine-miles roads. In the morning General Longstreet found the enemy in very large force in his front, pressing him so strongly that he considered it advisable not to send the brigade from General Huger's division, and later I ordered three additional brigades to his support. Meantime the enemy threatened General Whiting's position, which was not favorable for defense, and were evidently largely re-enforced and disposed to take the offensive. Reconnaissance made during the morning developed the fact that the enemy were strongly fortified in the position attacked by my division on the previous evening. This, coupled with the necessity of holding that portion of our line which was nearest the Chickahominy and covered Longstreet's left flank, induced me to direct General Whiting to assume more favorable ground a little in rear. This also brought his line in better relations with the troops of the centre, under General Magruder, and better secured the angle made by our line in front of New Bridge. Such was the condition of affairs upon the field at the time General Lee took command. The next morning (June 2), I was compelled by illness to leave the field. No official reports have as yet been made to me by subordinate commanders."

After informing General Lee of my determination to renew the attack, I directed my Chief of Staff, Major Jasper Whiting, to go at dawn to the Chickahominy, in the vicinity of New Bridge, and observe the movements of the enemy on that side. Major W. H. Stevens, Chief Engineer of Johnston's army, was requested to examine the enemy's position in front of General Whiting. Whatever may have been said by others at that time or since, in regard to the cutting of all communication between the Federals, on opposite sides of the river, because of the washing away of the bridges, I had reason that day to feel some anxiety in regard to the crossing of more troops from the north to the south side of the Chickahominy.

In reference to the fighting, June 1, already described, it may be of interest to know how it appeared through observations made from the Nine-miles road, interpreted by battle-field notes written to me that day by General Longstreet.

The first firing described by General Richardson, which he mistook for the beginning of a real attack, will be better understood in view of the orders given by me to Generals Longstreet and Whiting, and the description given by Captain Lemmon, of General Hood's staff. In his letter to me, already referred to, Captain Lemmon says: Hood's brigade was in the "front edge of the woods, with one regiment south of the railroad, Colonel Archer's Fifth Texas. Before daylight, on June 1, General Hood sent me to the left to find General Whiting and ask him for orders. I was with General Whiting and staff, in front of Hatton's brigade, when day broke, and the first gun of June 1 was fired, apparently at our group. . . . Beyond throwing our (Hood's) skirmishers well forward to the north side of the railroad, where they had lively firing for a time,* we did no fighting. I carried orders from General Hood to Colonel Archer to send men to his right and see how close he was to Hill and Longstreet, whom he reported about three-quarters of a mile from him."

Very early in the morning Major Jasper Whiting reported the movement of Federal troops and batteries passing down the north bank of the Chickahominy. About 6 A. M. General Whiting reported: "They are advancing a battery of six pieces beyond the wheat field of yesterday evening's fight—in front of where we stood last night. Hood is back in the woods, extending to the railroad in a swamp. My brigade partly in those woods and

---

* Hood's losses were 13 wounded.

partly in the large woods to the left. . . . You know that four of my brigades are without their commanders." At 6.30 A. M. he reported: "We will have to attack the position we tested last night, and that, I own, I don't like. Besides, it is just what the enemy wants. Heavy firing in advance of us and on the right." This from Whiting was in reply to instructions to be ready, when Longstreet's attack was fully developed, not only to make a diversion in his favor, but if necessary make a determined real attack in order to enable Longstreet to win.

I then wrote to General Whiting: "I fully appreciate your want of regular commanders for your four brigades, and if your force is increased by fresh troops, will have to send with them an officer of rank who will relieve you of a portion of your onerous duties." The "officer of rank," here alluded to, was General McLaws. I then intended, as soon as the attack by the right wing was made in full force, to bring up Griffith's and Semmes's brigades from the New Bridge road—put them in front line with the brigades of Hood and Whiting—put both of the latter brigades under Whiting's general control; give McLaws executive command of the four brigades in front line; place the brigades of Hampton, Hatton and Pettigrew in second line; take the executive control of the second line, and direct these seven brigades in action until A. P. Hill could reach the field with his division from the left wing of the army; leaving Magruder with four brigades to oppose any movement the Federals might make to cross the Chickahominy at or above New Bridge, in our rear and against Richmond.

A little later, General Whiting reported: "The musketry firing in advance is tremendous." But, so far, nothing had been observed from the Nine-miles road which indicated that any large portion of the right wing had commenced, in earnest, the movement in which Whiting had orders to co-operate. Whilst the musketry firing in particular localities had been for some time very heavy, it covered only a narrow front, and had not been of a character to satisfy me that Longstreet had put in close action more than a small portion of the forces under his control. It was clear that this attacking party had receded three or four hundred yards.

The first information I received from General Longstreet, was contained in the following note from him, dated, 8 o'clock, addressed to Major Whiting:

> * "HEADQUARTERS,
> June 1, 1862, 8 o'clock.
>
> "*Major:*
>
> "Yours of 6 is received. I have ordered a brigade of General Huger's, as agreed upon, to the support of General Whiting. Please send a guide for it.
>
> "J. LONGSTREET,
> "Major-General.

"Major WHITING."

The above note was received about 8.30 A. M. His delay in asking for a guide, even if one was really needed, annoyed me; and I was not specially pleased with his saying: "as agreed upon;" when, in point of fact, he was "ordered" to send a brigade. However, I merely said; "send a guide."

In the meantime Major Jasper Whiting's reports continued to show that some movement of the enemy was being made down the river on the north bank, and General Whiting had been ordered to throw back his right slightly, take position a little nearer the New Bridge fork of the Nine-miles road, and try to establish and keep up some sort of communication with Longstreet's left.

At 10.30 A. M., I wrote to General Longstreet: "The enemy are, from all accounts, crossing the river and concentrating below on this side. I have as yet heard nothing of Ripley's brigade or that from Huger's division. Ask Stuart if he cannot devise some means for keeping your left and Whiting's right in communication with each other. I have directed Whiting to take closer defensive relations with Magruder's troops. . . . That was absolutely necessary to enable a good defense to be made while you are pivoting on Whiting's position."

The following note was received from General Longstreet, before my note of 10.30 A. M., was dispatched:

---

* A *fac-simile* of this note is given on page 180.

* " HEADQUARTERS,
" June 1, 1862.

" *General :*

"The brigade cannot be spared. Every man except a brigade is engaged in action. As you are not fighting I did not send it nor can I spare it. If I find myself at any time so that I spare it I will send it. But I am now not able to do without it.

"Yours, respectfully,

"General SMITH." "J. LONGSTREET.

Almost at the same time the following, addressed to an officer of my staff, was received from General Longstreet:

† " JUNE 1.

" *Major :*

"Yours of to-day is received. The entire army seems to be opposed to me. I trust that some diversion may be made in my favor during these successive attacks, else my troops cannot stand it. The ammunition gives out too readily.

"Yours, respectfully,

"J. LONGSTREET,

"Major MELTON." "Major-General.

When the above two notes reached me I was about half a mile east of the New Bridge fork of the Nine-miles road in consultation with General McLaws, General Whiting and the Chief Engineer, Major Stevens. The latter had just returned from a reconnaissance in front of Whiting's command. Stevens reported that the position held by the enemy was a good one for defense, that it had been strengthened by fortifications, and was occupied by a strong force of infantry and artillery.

A few minutes only after the two foregoing notes from Longstreet had come to hand, I received from him the following:

‡ " HEADQUARTERS,
10 A. M., June 1.

" *General :*

"Can you re-enforce me, the entire army seems to be opposed to me ; we cannot hold out unless we get help. If we can fight

---

* A *fac-simile* is given on page 181.
† A *fac-simile* of this note is given on page 182.
‡ *Fac-simile* given on page 183.

together we can finish the work to-day, and Mc's time will be up. If I can't get help I fear that I must fall back.

"J. LONGSTREET.

"General SMITH."

That portion of his command which attacked the Federals at 6.30 A. M. had fallen back about two hours before the note of 10 A. M. was written. When I received it the firing had diminished materially, and it seemed that Longstreet was withdrawing from the fight, if not from the field. His first falling back had, to all appearance on the Nine-miles road, increased the gap between the right wing and Whiting's command.

The rapidly repeated appeals for help were so urgent that it seemed the engagement of the right wing that morning had been far more serious than was indicated by anything observed from the Nine-miles road. If that wing fell back much farther Whiting's right flank would be turned and he would probably be compelled to retire.

There were but two ways by which I could, at that time, possibly aid Longstreet in, what appeared from his notes to be, *his direful need*. One was by putting Whiting in close action, the other was to strip the Chickahominy Bluffs and send troops from there direct to Longstreet's assistance. I chose the latter method, and ordered about 5,000 men, then between the Mechanicsville and New Bridge roads, to move as rapidly as possible to the Williamsburg road, and report to General Longstreet on the battle-field. I directed that Ripley's brigade, which was expected in Richmond about that time, should move to the front on the Williamsburg, instead of on the Nine-miles road; and General McLaws was sent, in person, to General Longstreet to inform him of the re-enforcements ordered, to assure him that the whole army of the enemy was not in his front, and tell him that he must not fall back any farther, but drive the enemy; and, if possible, regain the ground he had lost.

In view of facts then existing, as already shown by both Federal and Confederate official reports of the actual fighting, it will be seen that I was, by the character of Longstreet's notes, as completely deceived in reference to the state of affairs in the right wing, on the morning of June 1, as General Johnston had been on the afternoon of May 31, by the note he received from Longstreet at 4 P. M. that day.

About 1 P. M., June 1, I received a note, from General McLaws, of which the following is a copy : *

" *General Smith:*

"I send a courier to bring General Cobb's brigade. Longstreet says he can hold his position with five thousand more men. He has now the same ground the enemy had yesterday. A drummer boy taken says that McClellan has gone to Washington to see after a man called Jackson.

"L. McL."

About 1.30 P. M. President Davis rode up to the headquarters near Old Tavern and aked for General Lee. On being told that I had not seen General Lee during the day, the President expressed so much surprise that I asked him if he had any special reason for supposing General Lee would then be there. To this he replied; Yes; and added that early in the morning he had ordered General Lee to take command of the army at once. This was the first intimation I received of the assignment of General Lee to the Army of Northern Virginia. I answered : In that case he will probably soon be here, and then invited the President to dismount and take a seat in the headquarters' office. He did so and chatted pleasantly upon a variety of common-place subjects; but made no allusion to anything pertaining to the state of affairs upon the field.

General Lee arrived about 2 P. M., and at once took command of the army. I commenced telling him what had occurred during the day. The President seemed to give some attention to what I said, especially to General Longstreet's notes asking for assistance. Whilst I was still explaining to General Lee the various occurrences of the day, the following note, dated 1.30 P. M., was received by me, from General Longstreet :

† " HEADQUARTERS,
"June 1, 1862, 1½ P. M.

" *General:*

"I have just received a note from Major Melton. I will give instructions to General Hill to extend his line of skirm-

---

Fac-simile on page 184.
† *Fac-simile* on pages 185-6-7.

ishers to the railroad. The next attack will be from Sumner's division. I think that if we can whip it we shall be comparatively safe from the advance of McClellan's army. I hope that those who were whipped yesterday will not appear again. The attack this morning was made at an unfortunate time. We had but little ammunition,* but we have since replenished our supply, and I sincerely hope that we may succeed against them in their next effort.

"Oh, that I had ten thousand men more.
"Yours, respectfully,
"J. LONGSTREET,
"Major-General Commanding.
"General G. W. SMITH,
"Commanding.

"Our line is already connected, General Stuart says, by cavalry vedettes.

"J. L."

When I finished reading the above note I handed it to General Lee. When he had read it, I asked him to hand it to President Davis. I then told General Lee that Longstreet was mistaken in supposing the whole Federal army was opposed to him. There was still a very large force in Whiting's immediate front; it was then certain that the great body of the two Federal corps on the north side of the river had made no important movement; and the 5,000 men ordered, several hours before, to move from the Chickahominy to the Williamsburg road, were closely approaching Longstreet's position. The danger to Richmond, if any, was not on the Williamsburg road.

After President Davis finished reading Longstreet's 1.30 P. M. note, he returned it to General Lee, and the latter handed it back to me. No comments were made upon it by either of them, but President Davis very soon rode away, leaving General Lee and myself in conference; everything at the front was quiet; no firing of any consequence had been heard since about 11 A. M.,

---

* Facts previously stated show that not one of the five Confederate brigades, engaged that day, had been in action the day before. It is, therefore, not at all probable that when "the attack this morning was made," these brigades could have "had but little ammunition." G. W. S.

and no movements of the enemy had been observed after that time.

General Lee made no adverse comment upon my management of the army, and gave me no orders then, or at any other time that day; between 4 and 5 P. M. he and I, with one of my couriers, went over to the Williamsburg road. The troops I had ordered from the Chickahominy had arrived, and were resting, under arms, a little in rear of where we found General Longstreet quietly talking with President Davis and several members of the Cabinet; after the ordinary greetings, General Longstreet, addressing me, began to explain the situation in the right wing; as soon as I caught the drift of his remarks, I said it would be better for him to address General Lee, who had relieved me as commander of the army.

During the time that we remained with General Longstreet all was quiet; no special information was obtained in regard to the events of that morning, or of the probable movements of the enemy; so far as I then knew, no questions of immediate importance were discussed. About 6 P. M. General Lee and myself returned to our respective headquarters on the Nine-miles road; with his approval I had ordered the troops that had been sent to Longstreet's assistance to return to the Chickahominy Bluffs.

General D. H. Hill's Official Report of Operations on the 1st of June.—He says, "At daylight next morning [he means daylight June 1] I learned that heavy re-enforcements had come up to the support of Keyes; Longstreet's, Huger's and my own divisions had opposed to us three Yankee corps—Keyes's, Sumner's, and Heintzelman's. We also learned that General G. W. Smith had been checked upon the Nine-miles road, and that no help could be expected in that direction; I therefore resolved to concentrate my troops around the captured works in the hope that the Yankees would attempt to retake them."

The tenor of General Hill's report leads to the inference that he controlled the whole right wing that day without guidance from any quarter. When my attention was first called to Hill's report in the published "Official Records," I wrote to him, on the 16th of June, 1885, and asked him to tell me what orders he received from General Longstreet at the battle of Seven Pines, on Sunday, June 1, 1862. In a letter to me, dated June 20, 1885, in reply to my question, he states: "General Hill says that he got no orders from General Longstreet on Sunday whatever."

In view of facts already established, these few and plain words, from General Hill, constitute the severest condemnation of General Longstreet's conduct as commander of the right wing of the Army of Northern Virginia, on the 1st of June, 1862.

Continuing his report, General Hill says: "Orders were accordingly given to the advance brigades, commanded by Pickett, Pryor and Wilcox, to draw in their extended lines and form near the late headquarters of General Casey. Before these orders were received a furious attack was made upon Generals Armistead, Mahone, Pickett, Pryor and Wilcox and their brigades on the left of the road."

General Hill omits to mention that Pickett's brigade came up that morning from its position far back on the railroad, and was almost immediately ordered, by Hill, to attack the enemy; then mistakenly supposed to be approaching in the woods north of Casey's former headquarters. Hill also omits to mention that Mahone's brigade came up from the Charles City road very soon after the arrival of Pickett's brigade; and Mahone was ordered, by Hill, to move into the same wood and attack the enemy. The official records do not show that Armistead's brigade received orders from Hill to advance to the attack, but there is abundant official testimony which shows he moved forward on the left of Pickett's brigade, between the latter and the railroad, and made a very determined attack on the Federal front line, to the Confederate right of the point where Mahone struck the same line. The accounts on both sides prove beyond question that the brigades of Pickett, Armistead and Mahone advanced to the attack. Two of them reached the Federal lines and made their blows felt; Pickett was checked before he reached Richardson's front line.

In omitting to state the fact that Pickett and Mahone were ordered to attack, and that Armistead went in with them; General Hill conveys the impression that these three brigades were attacked whilst holding definite positions in the Confederate lines. And, it seems that, misapprehension on the part of

General Hill in supposing the attack was commenced by the Federals moving against the brigades of Armistead, Mahone and Pickett resulted in Hill's doing grave injustice to Armistead's brigade, and in a less degree to Mahone's.

He adds: "Armistead's men fled early in the action, with the exception of a few heroic companies, with which that gallant officer maintained his ground against an entire brigade. Mahone withdrew his brigade without any orders. I sent up Colston's to replace him, but he did not engage the Yankees as I expected him to do. Pickett, Pryor and Wilcox received their orders to fall back after the firing began, and wisely resolved not to do so until the assault was repulsed. As soon as that was done Wilcox and Pryor withdrew, but Pickett held his ground against the odds of ten* to one for several hours longer, and only retired when the Yankees had ceased to annoy him."

As before stated, no official report or other account, from any one in that part of Armistead's brigade which advanced on Pickett's left can be found. But it is reasonable to infer—from the official reports and accounts of others, both on the Confederate and the Federal side—that Armistead's brigade, on the right of Mahone's, struck the Eighty-first Pennsylvania, of Howard's brigade, in Richardson's front line. That regiment was driven back in disorder. The action had then been kept up for an hour or more. Richardson's front line being thus broken, Armistead's brigade must have suffered heavy losses, because it was now met by fresh troops from Richardson's second line, by the fire of Birney's troops along the railroad, and by a charge from Birney's troops on the south side of the railroad. If General Hill had known these facts he certainly would not have so worded his official report as to give the impression that Armistead's brigade, in regular position, was attacked by the Federals, and "fled early in the action, with the exception of a few heroic companies, with which that gallant officer maintained his ground." No Confederates maintained their ground, for any length of time, in the position where Armistead's brigade met with disaster.

Mahone with two of his regiments attacked the left wing of

---

* But, see Federal "Official Records" already quoted.

French's brigade. The other regiment of Mahone's brigade had been at that time temporarily detached by General Hill. The latter regiment entered the woods later and after being for a time hotly engaged withdrew under mistaken orders. Mahone then withdrew the other two regiments and reformed the three regiments in the position from which they had been ordered to advance to the attack. Pickett was attacked by four Federal regiments only, and he withdrew after Colston and Mahone reenforced him. Wilcox withdrew his own brigade and Pryor's at once, on receipt of General Hill's positive written order. The enemy in their front had not been repulsed when these two brigades were withdrawn.

General Hill adds: "The Yankees were too prudent to attack us in position, and contented themselves for the balance of the day in a desultory fire of artillery, which hurt no one, and was only attended with the gratifying result of stampeding the amateur fighters and the camp plunderers from Richmond. The batteries of Maurin, Stribling and Watson had been added to those of the preceding day by General Longstreet and an occasional shot was fired in response to the Yankee artillery. The day was spent in removing 6,700 muskets and rifles in fine condition, ordnance, commissary and medical stores. Ten captured guns had been removed the night before. . . . General Longstreet sent me an order after dark to withdraw my whole command. The thirteen brigades were not got together until near midnight."

Withdrawal.—By half an hour after sunrise, June 2, the whole of the thirteen brigades had quietly filed by, and the rear guard "moved off, not a Yankee in sight or even a puff of smoke." Hill's division returned to their intrenchments on the Williamsburg road. Huger's division remained well out on that road, far in advance of Hill's intrenchments. Longstreet's division was ordered back to its camps on and near the Nine-miles road.

After the Federals discovered that the Confederates had withdrawn from the captured lines, that portion of Hooker's division which had been engaged the previous day took possession of Casey's earthworks during the morning; and that afternoon General Hooker made a reconnaissance a short distance in front of the line held by Casey's skirmishers before the action commenced. Hooker reported that "the enemy appeared to have a regiment of cavalry and three of infantry."

On the Nine-miles road, the division under Whiting remained in position closely confronting Sumner's corps at Fair Oaks Station. In a letter, dated June 10, 1862, addressed to the chief of my staff, General Whiting says: "The attention of the general commanding the army should be called at once to the condition of this division. Its effective strength is daily decreasing. Since Yorktown, with the exception of some four days during which it was encamped near Richmond, it has been constantly in contact with the enemy. It has fought two battles, the last an engagement of great severity, in which it suffered heavy loss, especially in officers, followed by two days of great hardship and privation. It now occupies an important position, where the service is exceedingly onerous, directly in the face of the enemy, with whom they are constantly engaged. They are in a swamp of an exceedingly unhealthy character, and to properly defend our centre, the labor is exhausting. . . . It is absolutely necessary that other troops relieve [this] the first division. If no other offers, the second division [that of A. P. Hill] might take its place. The Major-General, no doubt, is well aware of the condition of affairs, and although not now on duty, I appeal to his influence if it can be exerted. A copy of this is sent direct to the General commanding the army."

CHAPTER VII.

SUMMARY AND COMMENTS.

WHEN General J. E. Johnston, about noon, May 30, determined to order an attack upon the Federals in the vicinity of Seven Pines, the plan of striking a blow against their two corps on the south side of the Chickahominy river—and destroying them before they could be re-enforced by the three corps then on the north side of that stream—was not an inspiration of the moment; nor was it in any way connected with a high stage of water in the Chickahominy.

There was nothing in the mere locality of Seven Pines worth a contest on the part of the Confederates who had voluntarily yielded that position to the Federal advanced guard on the 24th of May. When the Federals, in force worth crushing, should come within easy striking distance of the Confederate army in front of Richmond, General Johnston intended to overwhelm that force, if possible, before it could receive assistance.

It is highly probable the attack would have been ordered earlier but for the fact that on the 27th the attention of the Confederate commander was suddenly called to the right flank of the Federals—on the north side of the Chickahominy—because of McDowell's movement, from Fredericksburg, to join McClellan.

On the night of the 28th, when General Johnston countermanded the order for attack upon Mechanicsville and Beaver Dam creek, General Longstreet urged that an attack should be made early next morning in the direction of Seven Pines. In reply General Johnston stated that the disposition of his forces, made when it was supposed McDowell was coming, was too strong on the extreme left to admit of immediate concentration against the Federal left wing—but, if McDowell did not promptly come on, a movement in full force would soon be made in the direction indicated. In all the discussions of this subject it was distinctly understood that promptness of action and determined fighting, by superior numbers on our side, were essential to complete Confederate success.

There are two main roads from Richmond to Seven Pines. On one of these—the Nine-miles road—there were three brigades of Longstreet's division, three and one-half miles from the city. The other three brigades of that division were not far from the point where that road leaves the suburbs. D. H. Hill's division was on the Williamsburg road two or three miles from Richmond; one brigade, however, being in observation well out on the Charles City road.

General Johnston intended that these two divisions should advance by the respective roads which they were already on and near. Hill was to initiate the attack on the Williamsburg road early in the morning, May 31; and that attack was to be promptly and closely supported by Longstreet's division moving into action on the Nine-miles road.

My division, then commanded by General Whiting, was on and near the Meadow Bridge road. In the written order, dated 9.15 P. M., May 30, sent by General Johnston, direct to General Whiting, the latter was instructed "to move by the Nine-miles road—coming as early as possible to the point at which the road to New Bridge turns off. Should there be cause of haste, General McLaws, on your approach, will be ordered to leave his ground for you that he may re-enforce General Longstreet."

Of the four brigades in McLaws's division, two were along the New Bridge road, and two were on the Chickahominy Bluffs, guarding the crossing of that stream between the New Bridge and Mechanicsville roads.

Huger's division, three brigades, had just arrived from Norfolk, and was in camp on Gilliss creek, near the eastern suburb of Richmond, not far north of the point where the Williamsburg road leaves the city. At 8.40 P. M., May 30, Huger was instructed to move his division, early next morning, on the Charles City road; relieve the brigade of D. H. Hill's division then in observation on that road; and "be ready" if an action should be begun on his left, to fall upon the enemy's left flank.

On May 31, General Johnston modified the above and gave Huger the following instructions: "It will be necessary for your progress to the front to conform at first to that of General Hill. If you find no strong body in your front, it will be well to aid General Hill; but then a strong reserve should be retained to cover our right."

At noon, May 30, when General Johnston determined to make the attack as early as possible next morning, it had not commenced to rain. He knew that two Federal corps were on the south side of the Chickahominy—extended from the vicinity of Seven Pines to Bottom's Bridge and White Oak Bridge. His information led him to believe that Sumner's corps had not yet crossed the river; but, on that point he was not well assured. It was, however, considered certain that Sumner would cross to the assistance of Keyes, in the vicinity of Seven Pines, as soon as the latter was attacked. There were two other Federal corps on the north side of the Chickahominy, extending from the vicinity of New Bridge to Mechanicsville. They might follow Sumner; or else move against Richmond, whilst the bulk of Johnston's army was engaged in the swamps around Seven Pines.

General Johnston believed that an attack by D. H. Hill, early in the morning, against the Federals on the Williamsburg road—promptly supported by the six brigades of Longstreet's division, moving on the Nine-miles road—would crush the Federals in the vicinity of Seven Pines before re-enforcements could reach them either from the direction of Bottom's Bridge, or from the north side of the river.

The attack which was to have been made by the six brigades of Longstreet's division, if successful, would have isolated the two Federal corps already on our side of the Chickahominy from the three corps believed to be on the north side of that stream—and thus cut McClellan's army in two.

To provide against Federal re-enforcements from the north side of the river, and other contingencies that might arise, General Johnston ordered my division, under Whiting, to move from the Meadow Bridge road, north of Richmond, and take position, as already stated; and, if this division could not reach that position in time, McLaws's division, "should there be cause of haste," would "re-enforce Longstreet."

When I reached General Johnston's headquarters—about 4.30 A. M.—I informed him that on the receipt of his order I had transmitted a copy of it to General Whiting, and directed him to move as soon as possible, and report to General Johnston. That I had learned from Whiting he had previously received the order from the Army Headquarters, and preparations for an early start had already been made. Whiting reported that the head of the division would move at dawn, and would be at the designated point on time.

General Johnston was then not only hopeful, but elated at the prospect of striking an effective blow early that morning against Keyes's corps. He had some anxiety in reference to movements the Federals from the north side of the Chickahominy might make against Richmond; but, with my division under Whiting, on the Nine-miles road, near its junction with the New Bridge road, he felt that Federal re-enforcements from the north side of the river, crossing below New Bridge, could be held in check long enough to enable the divisions of Longstreet and D. H. Hill to crush Keyes.

He informed me that he would, in person, be on the Nine-miles road, because the movements of the Federals on the north bank of the river could be better observed from that side; and he told me that, in case they made an attempt to cross above New Bridge, he would intrust to me the protection of the city whilst the mass of his army was engaged in the direction of Seven Pines.

Reasonable as were his expectations, at sunrise, May 31, they would have been much better founded if his orders had been given sooner. It was but little after midday, May 30, when he "resolved" to attack as early as possible next morning. There was ample time for Huger's division to move out on the Charles City road, relieve the brigade of D. H. Hill's division on that road, and for that brigade to unite with the three brigades of D. H. Hill's division on the Williamsburg road before, or very soon after, dark. There was nothing to prevent Longstreet's division from moving that afternoon, or early that night, to a point just within McLaws's line on the New Bridge road. And the division under Whiting might easily have been moved from the Meadow

Bridge road and closed up on Longstreet's division, on the Nine miles road, before midnight, May 30. Although these dispositions of the four divisions were not ordered, the state of things at sunrise—say 4.30 A. M.—seemed more than sufficiently favorable to justify General Johnston's elation at the prospect of crushing Keyes's corps very early that morning.

But, an order had already been given by General Longstreet, which would necessarily delay the attack far beyond the time General Johnston then expected it would occur. General D. H. Hill, in his official report, says: "I was directed by General Longstreet to move with my whole division at dawn on the Williamsburg road and to lead the attack on the Yankees. I was, however, directed not to move until relieved by Huger's division."

With this condition appended it was worse than idle for Longstreet to order Hill to move "at dawn" with his "whole division." Inevitable delay was caused by that order. If Huger had moved "at dawn" several hours would have elapsed before his division could reach the position held by one of Hill's brigades well out on the Charles City road; and additional time would be required for that brigade to cross the almost impracticable White Oak Swamp and reach the other brigades on the Williamsburg road.

But this delay, necessitated by the order now in question, was of but little moment compared with the delays which were caused by "Longstreet's misunderstanding" in regard to the direction in which his own division was to move into action; and his "mismanagement" after that division had been transferred from the Nine-miles road to the Williamsburg road.

Apparently unconscious of the pressing necessity for striking, in full force, a prompt and decisive blow against the Federals, isolated at Seven Pines, before they could be re-enforced; Longstreet very deliberately consumed much time in putting his own division in motion. One of his brigades, if not more, took their baggage wagons and camp equipage with them. When they did start, instead of moving towards the enemy, at Seven Pines, his division was directed to Huger's camp, on the banks of Gilliss creek, near the east suburb of Richmond. Before leaving camp

Longstreet's own troops delayed the division under Whiting; at Gilliss creek they took precedence of, and delayed, Huger's division.

Between 10 and 11 A. M. Longstreet had about 30,000 men under his control, on the Williamsburg and Charles City roads, the great body of them being near the junction of those roads. At that time and place, by authority of General Johnston, he took command of Huger's division, in addition to his own and that of D. H. Hill. At 1 P. M. Hill's four brigades advanced to attack. After more than two hours' very hard fighting, these four brigades, unaided, captured Casey's earthworks. In the meantime Longstreet held six brigades on the Charles City road—south of the White Oak Swamp, where there was no enemy—five of those brigades being near the junction of that road with the Williamsburg road. He held Pickett's brigade far back on the Richmond and York River Railroad; and he ordered two brigades to move up on the Williamsburg road, "to support Hill if need be."

Long before Hill's four brigades captured Casey's earthworks Sumner had crossed to the south side of the Chickahominy and was hurrying to the assistance of his friends; and the head of Heintzelman's corps had come up from Bottom's Bridge to the Federal third line of defense—within supporting distance of Keyes—before Hill's attack commenced.

General D. H. Hill, in his official report, says: "My division had beaten Casey's division and all the re-enforcements brought him. . . . It was desirable, however, to press the Yankees as closely as possible. I therefore sent back to General Longstreet and asked for another brigade. In a few minutes the magnificent brigade of R. H. Anderson came to my support." This was about 3.30 P. M. The brigade Longstreet sent to Hill's assistance went into action at 4 P. M. At that time General Johnston received a note from General Longstreet asking for help and complaining of Johnston's "slowness."

The wrong impression conveyed by that note was the cause of trouble on the Nine-miles road, which need not be repeated here. It is enough now to say that one of the five brigades on that road was sent by General Johnston direct to Longstreet's assistance;

and the four other brigades of the division, under Whiting, not only held in check the re-enforcements, under Sumner, sent to assist Keyes and Heintzelman, but they held "cut off"—from the forces opposed to Longstreet—four regiments and a battery of Couch's division; and incidentally prevented Birney's brigade, of Heintzelman's corps, from re-enforcing Keyes at a critical time.

When Longstreet complained of Johnston's "slowness" he started five brigades on the Charles City road marching and countermarching on that road, near its junction with the Williamsburg road, and kept them there so that they did not reach the Williamsburg road, at a point far in rear of the fighting, until 5 P. M.

At that time the head of Sumner's column went into action north of Fair Oaks Station; and Kearney's troops had been for fully an hour pressing back the right of D. H. Hill's division from the second abatis. The five brigades from the Charles City road reached the front too late to be put in action that day.

But General D. H. Hill says in his official report: "Kemper's brigade was now sent me by General Longstreet, and directed by me to move directly to the support of Rodes. This brigade, however, did not engage the Yankees, and Rodes's men were badly cut up." The brigade that Longstreet placed far back on the railroad was held in that position until the next day. So, out of thirteen brigades in the right wing, under the control of General Longstreet, he succeeded in putting five brigades in close action, May 31; and of these only one was from his own division, in which there were six brigades.

Yet, in his letter, June 7, 1862, to General Johnston, Longstreet says: "The failure of complete success on Saturday [May 31], I attribute to the slow movements of General Huger's command. This threw perhaps the hardest part of the battle upon my own poor division." In commenting on that letter D. H. Hill says: "Longstreet was not on the field at all on the 31st of May, and did not see any of the fighting. But he ought to have known that I got no assistance from him except the brigade of R. H. Anderson."

In a letter addressed to me, May 18, 1885, General D. H.

Hill says: "I cannot understand Longstreet's motive in coming over to the Williamsburg road, nor can I understand Johnston's motive in shielding him."

Without entering upon questions of *motive*, attention is called to the fact that a portion of the only brigade of Longstreet's own division that was put in close action, May 31, was sent back from the Williamsburg road to the Nine-miles road, near Fair Oaks Station, after 3.30 p. m., by D. H. Hill. The service done by the two regiments under Colonel Jenkins, after 4 p. m., is sufficient evidence of what would have been the probable effect had Longstreet's division gone promptly into action on the Nine-miles road, on D. H. Hill's left, as General Johnston certainly intended. Longstreet himself sent one brigade back from the Williamsburg road to the railroad; but he held it there to "repel any advance of the enemy up that road;" instead of sending it forward into the fight.

In a letter dated June 28, 1862, addressed to me, General Johnston says: "I received information of Longstreet's misunderstanding (which may be my fault as I told you at the time) while his troops were moving to the Williamsburg road, and sent to Longstreet to send three brigades by the Nine-miles road, if they had not marched so far as to make the change involve a serious loss of time."

I have no recollection of his telling me that the "misunderstanding" may have been his own fault. I know that he was greatly surprised and annoyed by the information that Longstreet's division was not on the Nine-miles road. And he was strongly inclined to the opinion that my aide must have been mistaken.

But it may be that General Johnston felt it might be his "fault" that it did not occur to him—whilst placing Longstreet in control of the three divisions of the right wing—to order him not to bring back to Huger's camp near Richmond the three brigades of his own division, which were already three and a half miles out from that city, on one of the two main roads leading to Seven Pines; not to march his whole division to that camp; not to take precedence of Huger's division, at that point; not to place two brigades of Huger's division and three brigades of his own division near the junction of the Williamsburg and Charles City roads and keep them there until 3.30 P. M.; not to march and countermarch these five brigades on the Charles City road, where there was no enemy; and finally at 5 P. M.— by crossing the White Oak Swamp—bring the head of this column of five brigades to a point on the Williamsburg road far in rear of the fighting that had then been raging for four hours; and not to place one of his brigades back on the railroad to "repel any advance of the enemy up that road" and keep it there whilst the contest against the Federal left wing was raging from 1 P. M. until dark.

In short, it may have been General Johnston's "fault" that it did not occur to him to order Longstreet to put more than one of the six brigades of his own division into close action, to support D. H. Hill's four brigades, in the effort to crush and, if possible, destroy Keyes's corps before it could be re-enforced.

In this connection it is well to glance at some of General Longstreet's statements in regard to his understanding of General Johnston's plan; of which he claims to speak "from accurate knowledge." He says: "The plan was to turn your [the Federal] left at daylight by throwing Huger's division, by a passable route for infantry, to your left and rear. As the head of his column passed the swamp, D. H. Hill was to be ready, and I was to advise him to make the attack vigorously. Huger did not reach the field. At 1 o'clock D. H. Hill proposed to bring on the battle, and it was agreed to under the impression that Huger would be there surely by the time we were warmed up into actual battle." *

"Our plan was, as you stated, to turn your left by moving Huger's command across the head of White Oak Swamp; that to be followed by the attack of General D. H. Hill, on the Williamsburg road, which was to be supported, if need be, by my command; the command on the Nine-miles road following Hill's movements. As you say in your article, Johnston's plan was

---

* General Longstreet, in letter dated July 17, 1874, addressed to General G. W. Mindil.

faultless, and, in my judgment at the time, was the only plan that could be approved by a military mind."*

However "accurate" General Longstreet's knowledge of Johnston's plan may have been "at the time," he has now grossly misstated it. The written instructions given by General Johnston show that Huger's division was not ordered to turn the Federal left at daylight; and the order given to Whiting shows that the command on the Nine-miles road was not to follow Hill's movements. Moreover, the records show conclusively that D. H. Hill was not to be held back until Huger's command had crossed the White Oak Swamp and had turned the Federal left.

When Whiting found his march obstructed by Longstreet's troops, he became impatient at the delay and wrote to General Johnston. In reply he was informed by the latter, "Longstreet will precede you." The plain meaning of which is: Longstreet's division was to precede the division under Whiting, on the Nine-miles road. General McLaws was guarding the New Bridge crossing and the Bluffs of the Chickahominy. Yet, General Longstreet would have it believed that, "Should there be cause of haste General McLaws" "will be ordered to leave his ground," "that he may re-enforce General Longstreet;" the latter being on the Williamsburg road, and expected only to support D. H. Hill, "if need be;" and Hill to be held back until Huger's division had crossed the White Oak Swamp and turned the Federal left flank!

No such *preposterous* "plan" as that attributed by Longstreet to Johnston could ever have been evolved, out of the plain facts, if General Johnston had permitted it to be "generally known" that Longstreet "misunderstood" the direction in which his own division was to move into action.

In speaking of the results of the fighting, May 31, General Johnston says: "General Hill pursued the enemy toward Bottom's Bridge more than a mile; then, night being near, he gathered his troops and reformed them, facing to the east, as they had been fighting. The line thus formed crossed the Williamsburg road at right angles. The left, however, was thrown back

---

* General Longstreet to General G. W. Mindil, 1874.

to face Sumner's corps at Fair Oaks. In an hour or two Longstreet's and Huger's division, whom it had not been necessary to bring into action, came into this line under General Longstreet's orders."*

"The troops in position to renew the battle on Sunday were, at Fair Oaks, on the Federal side, two divisions and a brigade; one of the divisions, Richardson's, had not been engaged, having come upon the field about, or after, nightfall. On the Confederate side, ten brigades in Smith's and Magruder's divisions, six of which were fresh, not having fired a shot. On the Williamsburg road four Federal divisions, three of which had fought and been thoroughly beaten—one, Casey's, almost destroyed. On the Confederate side, thirteen brigades, but five of which had been engaged on Saturday—when they defeated the three Federal divisions that were brought against them successively. After nightfall, Saturday, the two bodies of Federal troops were completely separated from the two corps of their right, beyond the Chickahominy, by the swollen stream, which had swept away their bridges, and Sumner's corps at Fair Oaks was six miles from those of Heintzelman and Keyes, which were near Bottom's Bridge; but the Confederate forces were united on the front and left flank of Sumner's corps. Such advantage of position and superiority of numbers would have enabled them to defeat that corps had the engagement been renewed on Sunday morning, before any aid could have come from Heintzelman, after which his troops, in the condition to which the action of the day before had reduced them, could not have made effectual resistance." †

"At half-past six o'clock [May 31] . . . . I announced to my staff officers that each regiment must sleep where it might be standing when the contest ceased for the night, to be ready to renew it at dawn next morning. About seven o'clock I received a slight wound in the right shoulder from a musket shot, and a few moments after was unhorsed by a heavy fragment of shell which struck my breast." ‡

---

* "Johnston's Narrative," page 136.
† "Johnston's Narrative," page 141.
‡ "Johnston's Narrative," page 138.

In his official report, General Johnston says: "About sunset" "I was carried from the field, and Major-General G. W. Smith succeeded to the command. He was prevented from renewing his attack on the enemy's position next morning by the discovery of strong intrenchments not seen on the previous evening."

It is not proposed to discuss at any length what he says "prevented" me, as commander of the army, "from renewing" the attack which he insists I made on Sumner, May 31. But, in this connection, it is well to notice that, in my official report it is stated: "General Longstreet was directed to push his successes of the previous day as far as practicable, pivoting his movement upon the position of General Whiting, on his left. The latter was directed to make a diversion in favor of General Longstreet's real attack."

Utterly ignoring that statement of mine—made to him in an official report—he claims that such advantages were gained before he was disabled, as to make it certain that three Federal corps, on the south side of the Chickahominy, would have been destroyed, June 1, if he could have retained command of his army that day.

Upon examination of the data on which he bases this claim, it is found from the official records—the detailed reports of the fighting commanders, made at the time—that General Johnston's statements, in reference to the positions occupied by the contending forces are, to say the least, very inaccurate. D. H. Hill's division did not pursue the enemy from Seven Pines towards Bottom's Bridge. On the contrary, that division was checked at the second abatis; and its right was forced back to Casey's earthworks—from which it was withdrawn before dark—and bivouacked with the rest of that division, more than a mile west of Seven Pines, instead of being in line of battle more than a mile east of that point, as stated by General Johnston.

The five brigades, from the Charles City road, that reached the front too late to be put in action that day, went into bivouac, with Kemper's brigade, in the open ground around the captured works. Pickett's brigade passed the night far back on the railroad; Mahone's brigade was in observation on the Charles City road; and Colonel Jenkins's command remained, for a few hours only, at the point—about half a mile east of Seven Pines—where it had ceased fighting at dark. During the night, the brigades of Wilcox and Pryor relieved Colonel Jenkins's command. The latter then retired to the Federal camps at Seven Pines; and the two relieving brigades bivouacked on the Williamsburg road; the head of the column being on the ground where Jenkins ceased fighting.

Yet General Johnston says D. H. Hill's division was in line of battle across the Williamsburg road, a mile east of Seven Pines; and would have it believed that "Longstreet's and Huger's division" both passed the night in line of battle, facing north, on the immediate left flank, and overlapping the rear of Sumner's corps; which, he says, was drawn up in line facing nearly west. And he places ten Confederate brigades, "six of which were fresh, not having fired a shot," "in position," in front of Sumner, "to renew the battle on Sunday."

There were but five brigades in front of Sumner, in position to renew the battle. One of these brigades (Hood's) was "fresh, not having fired a shot;" because it had been sent, by General Johnston, direct to Longstreet's assistance—reached Longstreet's troops after D. H. Hill's division had ceased fighting at the second abatis, and being recalled, arrived at Fair Oaks a little after the fighting north of that point ended.

Of the five brigades, in Magruder's command, which General Johnston says were confronting Sumner: one was near the Mechanicsville road, guarding the crossing of the Chickahominy; two were on the bluffs between that road and the vicinity of New Bridge; and two were at the latter point and along the New Bridge road. The only other brigade of Magruder's command was on the Meadow Bridge road. Magruder's troops were the only forces guarding the line of the Chickahominy.

Whilst General Johnston insists that "the Confederates were united on the front and left flank of Sumner's corps;" he says that the latter "was six miles from those of Heintzelman and Keyes." But, in point of fact, early on the morning of June 1, the right of Kearney's division, of Heintzelman's corps, overlapped the left of Sumner's corps in line of battle along the railroad; two brigades of Kearney's division were in the rifle-pits of the third line of defense, on the north side of the Williamsburg road, within supporting distance of the leading brigade; Keyes's corps was in the third line of defense south of the Williamsburg road; and half of Hooker's division of Heintzelman's corps, was a few hundred yards in rear of Keyes. The other half of Hooker's division occupied the fortifications at Bottom's Bridge and at White Oak Bridge.

With the exception of these guards at the bridges, the three Federal corps, on the south side of the Chickahominy, were practically united early on the morning of June 1, and were not so thoroughly cut off from the two corps on the north side of that stream as General Johnston seems to suppose. General J. G. Barnard, Chief Engineer of McClellan's army, in his official report, says: "At 8.15 A.M. (June 1), the pontoon bridge at the site of New Bridge was complete and passable to infantry, cavalry and artillery." The railroad bridge was intact, throughout the freshet, and had been arranged for the prompt passage of all arms of the service. "About noon the upper trestle bridge was practicable for infantry. It was not till night that a practicable bridge for infantry was obtained at the lower trestle bridge."

It is true that eight regiments of raw troops in Casey's division, after more than two hours of very hard fighting, were thrown into great confusion whilst moving in retreat, under deadly fire, across the abatis in their rear. Finding the earthworks of the second line occupied, a large portion of these raw troops continued to retreat; some of them as far as the Chickahominy. But they were rallied, and placed in the third line of defense early next morning. Five regiments of Casey's division remained on the field during the contest for Couch's line, and there is no reason to believe they were demoralized—much less "almost destroyed." Two brigades of Kearney's division were elated at their success; and the other brigade of that division was not in action May 31. Couch's division was in fairly good condition; and Hooker's division had not yet been in the fight.

General Johnston assumes a good deal when he says the left wing of McClellan's army, "in the condition to which the action of the day before had reduced them, could not have made effectual resistance;" and he is far beyond the record when he says there was a gap of six miles between the left wing of the Federal army and Sumner's corps!

His claim that the three Federal corps on the south side of the Chickahominy would have been destroyed on the 1st of June, if he had not been disabled on the 31st of May, will be judged in connection with what he had succeeded in doing against one corps, isolated at Seven Pines, during more than twenty-four hours from the time he "resolved" to make the attack.

In his "Narrative" he says: "An hour or two later [than noon, May 30], orders were given for the concentration of twenty-three of our twenty-seven brigades against McClellan's left wing."* When he was wounded a little before sunset May 31, he had put only five brigades in action against that wing!

In reference to the actual fighting on the 1st of June, the official reports of Generals Sumner and Richardson and their brigade and regimental commanders, show, beyond question, that Richardson's division was very rudely assaulted about 6.30 A. M. His front line was severely shaken, one regiment was driven back, and did not again come into close action. The contest continued an hour or more before the front line was broken. That line was not only restored by the advance of fresh troops, but these, together with Birney's brigade, of Kearney's division, of Heintzelman's corps, assailed the attacking Confederates in front and flank, and repulsed them. Advancing through the dense and tangled wood, four Federal regiments, three of Richardson's division and one of Birney's brigade, ran against a Confederate force, in an abatis, in front of the left wing of French's brigade, about 300 yards south of the railroad. The contest continued at this point for two hours or more; and the four Federal regiments were withdrawn to the positions from which they had advanced. The losses in Richardson's division in killed and wounded were 751; in Birney's brigade 197. Total Federal killed and wounded, on that part of the field, 948.

The Confederate accounts, although far less explicit than those of the Federals, show, beyond reasonable doubt, that Richardson's division was attacked by two Confederate brigades only. The position, in front of the left wing of French's brigade, 300

---

* Johnston's Narrative, page 132.

yards south of the railroad, was held by a Confederate brigade which was not engaged in the attack on Richardson's line. The losses in that brigade were 350 killed and wounded.

One of the brigades that attacked Richardson lost 338; the losses in the other brigade (Armistead's) are not stated; but, judging from its position on the field—and the flank as well as front attack to which it was subjected by fresh troops, after it had broken Richardson's front line—it is probable that the losses in this brigade were very great. It is, therefore, safe to assume that the Confederate losses in Richardson's front were equal to, if not greater than, those of the Federals—and that the killed and wounded on the two sides, in this affair, were about 2,000, not including losses on other parts of the field that day.

In his "History of the Army of the Potomac," Swinton says: "General Johnston has frequently expressed to the writer his amazement at the swelling bulk assumed by the 'skirmish' of the 1st, . . . and asserts that nothing more severe than an affair of the rear guard took place"!

Between 7 and 8 A. M., June 1, the five regiments of Sickles's brigade and two New Jersey regiments—all under the command of General Hooker—were sent forward on, and on the north side of, the Williamsburg road, to aid Richardson. The Confederates that were struck by Hooker had taken no part in the fighting against, or near, Richardson's lines. They were the brigades of Wilcox and Pryor, both under control of General Wilcox.

When the firing commenced against Richardson, General Wilcox, whilst awaiting orders, arranged his troops, ready for any emergency.

General Hooker, in his official report, after describing his first movements, and the initial firing, says: "Directions were given to advance with the bayonet, when the enemy were thrown into wild confusion, throwing away their arms, hats and coats, and broke through the forest in the direction of Richmond."

In his official report, General Wilcox, after describing the commencement of the action, says: "The Nineteenth Mississippi had already repulsed the enemy in its front, the other troops doing well, and the engagement now raging furiously was going on as well as could be desired ; but just at this time an order in writing was sent to me to withdraw my command, which was instantly done."

He adds: " Pryor's brigade was not engaged on the 31st, but acted well on the second day, and yielded reluctantly to the order to withdraw." In the light furnished by Wilcox's report, it is clearly seen that the picture given by General Hooker, illustrating the effect of his "bayonet charge," is too highly colored.

General D. H. Hill, in his official report, says that he resolved to concentrate the thirteen brigades of the right wing of the Confederate army " around the captured works, in the hope that the Yankees would attempt to retake them," and adds, they " were too prudent to attack us in position, and contented themselves for the balance of the day in a desultory fire of artillery, which hurt no one, and was only attended with the gratifying result of stampeding the amateur fighters and the camp plunderers from Richmond."

There was another Federal so-called "bayonet charge" before the fighting ended. In his official report General French, commanding brigade, says: " The second and third lines of the division [Richardson's] having interposed in front of my left wing, I moved the right wing, consisting of the Sixty-sixth New York and Fifty-seventh New York, . . . in a direction at right angles to the first line of battle, to feel the left and rear of the enemy's flank. After penetrating the swamps and thicket about three-fourths of a mile the skirmishers of the Sixty-sixth encountered the Forty-first Virginia. A heavy fire being opened upon them, followed by a charge with the bayonet, the enemy broke and precipitately fled, when my brigade, occupying the ground, thus conquered, notwithstanding its losses in the battle, remained upon the field unbroken and exultant."

The Sixty-sixth New York formed the right of French's line, and it was the only regiment of his brigade which was on the north side of the railroad. The Fifty-seventh New York, on the left of the Sixty-sixth, does not seem to have participated in this " bayonet charge." The losses in the Fifty-seventh were, three killed and fifteen wounded. The casualties in the latter regiment probably occurred before it advanced from the original front line of Richardson's division. In that line it was contiguous to the left wing of French's brigade where the Confederate attack was made. The credit of the bayonet charge, "before which the enemy broke and precipitately fled," must be awarded exclusively to the Sixty-sixth New York.

The Fifty-third Virginia, Colonel Tomlin, of Armistead's brigade, Huger's division, was detained, during the night, May 31, by General Longstreet, as a guard to his headquarters. On being relieved from that duty, Colonel Tomlin, under instructions from General Armistead, moved his regiment into the woods, north of Casey's redoubt, in search of the left of the Ninth Virginia. In that search, Colonel Tomlin says his regiment "came up with the Forty-first Virginia, marching directly toward us. From this direction we received a constant fire, which we returned until some of our officers, recognizing some of the officers of the Forty-first Virginia," "an order was given by the Major of the regiment for the left wing to retreat." "Friends and enemies were so indiscriminately mixed up together that it was most advisable to return to the open field. We returned slowly to the field, apprehending more danger from friends than the enemy. We again reformed and reported for duty to Major-General Hill." The latter assigned the regiment to position in the open ground around the redoubt.

It thus appears that, whilst the Fifty-third Virginia was moving in the densely tangled wood under General Armistead's orders, to form line on the left of the Ninth Virginia; the Forty-first Virginia, which had been repulsed in the attack on Richardson's line, was moving back, under General Mahone's order, to reform in the open field. These two Virginia regiments commenced firing into each other; and, whilst thus engaged, before the mistake was rectified, the Sixty-sixth New York, from the north side of the railroad, came upon the ground, "conquered" it "by a charge with the bayonet," and "remained upon the field [in the dense and tangled wood] unbroken and exultant," "notwithstanding its losses in the battle;" which were 1 man killed and 5 wounded!

A little later, General D. H. Hill sent Mahone and Colston to Pickett's assistance in the defensive position held by the latter in the abatis in front of French's left wing, about 300 yards south of the railroad. At that time Pickett's brigade was being attacked by the Fifth New Hampshire regiment only. On the approach of Mahone and Colston the Fifth New Hampshire withdrew from Pickett's front, and resumed its place, in Richardson's second line, north of the railroad.

After sending back his wounded, Pickett, by General Hill's order, quietly withdrew his own brigade and those of Mahone and Colston; all three brigades taking position in the open ground around Casey's earthworks, where no one was molested during the remainder of the day.

Although Pickett's brigade was attacked by but four Federal regiments in all, he made frantic appeals for help, which was finally sent to him by General Hill. In his official report, after detailing these appeals, Pickett says, "the last message [to Hill] being that if he would send more troops and some ammunition to me we would drive the enemy across the Chickahominy; and I have always believed this would have been done but for the misfortune which happened to our General [J. E. Johnston] on the previous evening. Had he not been wounded, and been on the field with us, the result would have been entirely different. I do not mean to cast any blame on the brave and heroic Hill, for after the fall of the master spirit [Johnston] there seemed to be no head, and Hill, I know, was bothered and amazed with countermanding orders. No assistance, no demonstration was given or made from the other side of the railroad. A most perfect apathy seemed to prevail; not a gun was fired, and I subsequently learned from Brigadier-General Hood that he saw the enemy pouring his forces across the railroad not more than 600 or 800 yards in his front and concentrating their attack on me; that one piece of artillery placed in the railroad cut would have stopped this and drawn their attention to his front, but he said he had orders to make no movement, but to wait for orders. A forward movement then by the left wing of our army [he means the division under Whiting] would have struck the enemy in flank—at any rate, have stopped their concentration."

Without dwelling upon what General Pickett says would have been the result if General Johnston had been in command that day, or commenting here on what he says he knows about Hill's having been "bothered and amazed with countermanding orders," or discussing at present his statement that " a most perfect apathy seemed to prevail" on "the other side of the railroad"; it may be well to call attention to the fact that the only enemy Hood saw, " pouring his forces across the railroad ", was the Sixty-sixth New York. So far from " concentrating " on Pickett, whose defensive position was in front of French's left wing, the regiment Hood saw constituted the right of French's right wing; and General French says he moved that regiment " in a direction at right angles to the first line of battle." Moving in that direction the Sixty-sixth New York could not "concentrate" on Pickett.

If the latter really needed help when the Fifth New Hampshire was the only force "concentrating" against him, there were at least eight brigades of the Confederate right wing then in position around Casey's captured earthworks; and all of them, if necessary, could easily and quickly have been sent to Pickett's assistance.

In a letter to General G. W. Mindil, 1874, General Longstreet says: "I do not remember to have heard of any fighting on the second day except a sharp skirmish reported by General Pickett as he was retiring under the orders of General Lee, to resume our former position."

Between 2 and 3 A. M., June 1, General Longstreet was ordered to renew the attack as early as possible that morning; and fight toward the north, rather than attempt to drive the enemy any farther east. About 11 A. M., I received, in rapid succession, three notes from him. In the first he said: " The brigade cannot be spared. Every man except a brigade is in action. As you are not fighting, I did not send it." In the second: " I trust that some diversion may be made in my favor during these successive attacks else my troops cannot stand it. The ammunition gives out too readily." In the third: " We cannot hold out unless we get help. If we can fight together we can finish the work to-day, and Mc.'s time will be up. If I can't get help I fear I must fall back."

These, rapidly repeated, urgent appeals for help indicated that the engagement of the right wing had been far more serious than I had reason to believe from observations made on the Nine-miles road during the morning; and I inferred from those notes that the right wing under Longstreet was in pressing need of prompt and effective assistance.

In giving due weight to his complaints that I was not fighting, I knew there was still a large Federal force on the north side of the river, and there was a strong body of infantry and five batteries in front of Whiting, which had not disturbed Longstreet. If Whiting attacked the forces in his front he would have to pass over 800 or 1,000 yards of open ground, in deep mud. If he succeeded in carrying their position, this would not necessarily diminish the pressure already brought against Longstreet. Moreover there was a wide gap between Whiting's right and Longstreet's left. In ordering Longstreet to fight towards the north, and pivot his movement on Whiting's position; it was intended that the right wing should close that gap. This had not been done. On the contrary, when the Confederate firing receded from the railroad, about 8 A. M., the gap seemed to be increased. Whiting's left flank was in the air, with no support nearer than the force guarding the crossing at New Bridge and along the New Bridge road.

In view of Longstreet's peril, as depicted in his three notes, just received, I ordered 5,000 men, who were then guarding the Chickahominy between the New Bridge and Mechanicsville roads, to move at once to the Williamsburg road. Ripley's brigade, which was just arriving in Richmond, was ordered to move out on that road, instead of coming on the Nine-miles road; and General McLaws was sent to Longstreet to inform him of the re-enforcements ordered; assure him that the whole army of the enemy was not in his front; and tell him that he must not fall back any farther, but drive the enemy; and, if possible, regain the ground he had lost.

About 1 P. M. I received a note from McLaws stating: "Longstreet says he can hold his position with 5,000 more men. He has now the same ground the enemy held yesterday." About 2 P. M. General Lee reached the headquarters of the army, and at once took command. Within a few minutes after General Lee arrived I received the following from General Longstreet, dated 1.30 P. M.: "The next attack will be from Sumner's division. I think that if we can whip it we shall be comparatively safe from the advance of McClellan's army. I hope that those who were whipped yesterday will not appear again. . . . I sincerely hope that we may succeed against them in their next effort. Oh, that I had 10,000 men more."

The originals of General Longstreet's battle-field notes, June 1, 1862, in his own handwriting, are now in my possession. They must stand, in all their significance, as a part of the record he then made; even, if he does say, in 1874: " I do not remember to have heard of any fighting on the second day except a sharp skirmish reported by General Pickett as he was retiring, under the orders of General Lee, to resume our former position."

In his letter to General Mindil, General Longstreet adds: "About 10 A. M. General Lee was assigned to command and rode out on the Nine-miles road, saw General Smith, took command, and came with General Smith to the Williamsburg road. There we discussed the matter of renewed attack. I favored another effort to turn your [the Federal] left. Smith opposed it, and gave as his reason the strength of your lines, which he claimed to have examined, and I was forced to yield my opinions, in consequence of his knowledge of superior position on your side."

General Lee took command after 2 P. M. Between 4 and 5 P. M. he and I crossed over to the Williamsburg road. The troops that had been ordered from the Chickahominy Bluffs had arrived, and were in line, a little in rear of where we found General Longstreet. All was quiet, and had been since about 11 A. M., except occasional firing of cannon. I have no recollection of General Longstreet's having proposed to turn the Federal left, or make any other offensive movement. Such a suggestion from him, in view of the tenor of his notes to me that day—more especially the one dated 1.30 P. M.—would certainly have made an impression on my mind. It would clearly have indicated in him a wonderful and sudden change of heart. I had no knowledge of "the strength of the enemy's lines" in Longstreet's front; or on the Federal left; which he says he proposed to make "another effort to turn;" neither did I claim to have such knowledge.

General Longstreet says farther: "Attack was not renewed on the 1st of June, because Johnston had been wounded and had been obliged to leave the field. Smith, the next in rank, had been taken quite sick, but would not give up. He was therefore slow in organizing for renewed attack, and before he did so arrange General Lee was announced as commander of the army. As he had not been with the army the previous day, he was not prepared to conduct the continuance of the battle; so the troops were withdrawn to their original positions in the afternoon and evening."

The troops were not withdrawn during the afternoon and evening. I was not "taken quite sick" until eighteen hours after General Lee assumed command of the army. When I succeeded in communicating with General Longstreet, about 2 A. M., June 1, the "organizing" necessary "for renewed attack" had been "arranged;" except in the right wing under Longstreet. It is not proposed to recapitulate here the events of that day, or to dwell again upon the notes Longstreet addressed to me, or to discuss now what might have occurred if Johnston had not been wounded. It may, however, be well to state that, with full knowledge of the contents of Longstreet's battle-field notes, General Lee might well feel "he was not prepared to conduct the continuance of the battle" after 5 P. M.; even if Longstreet had proposed to make "another effort" to turn the Federal left.

To me the most astounding revelation connected with these events is the fact that Longstreet, after ordering every brigade in the right wing of the army to report to D. H. Hill; gave Hill no orders whatever that day, until after dark. As the regular commander of the three divisions in that wing, General Longstreet was given positive orders to renew the fight, and general instructions in regard to the direction of the fighting. He virtually abdicated command; failed to transmit the orders he had received; kept those facts from me; wrote the battle-field notes of which *fac-similes* are given; and would now have it believed that he was anxious to renew the fighting, but was overruled "in consequence" of my opposition!

General D. H. Hill, in his official report, says: "General Longstreet sent me an order after dark to withdraw my whole command. The thirteen brigades were not got together until near midnight. . . . We regained our own intrenchments by sunrise."

In the latter sentence General Hill refers only to his own division. Longstreet's division had no intrenchments. On the 30th of May three brigades of his division were on the Nine-miles road about three miles in rear of McLaws's line on the New Bridge road; and his three other brigades—near the point at which the Nine-miles road leaves the city—were several miles in rear of Magruder's line on the Chickahominy.

On the morning of June 2 Longstreet's division returned to their camps, on and near the Nine-miles road, from which, on the 31st of May, they should not have been transferred to the Williamsburg and Charles City roads.

General Pickett, in his official report, says: "General Hill sent for me about 1 o'clock at night, or rather, morning of June 2, and I went to the redoubt in search of him and still farther on toward our picket line. General Hill gave me special orders to cover [the] withdrawal of the troops with my brigade. . . . I had formed my line of battle, two regiments on each side of [the] road, some little distance in our rear of the redoubt. The whole of our force filed past by half an hour after sunrise. I then leisurely moved off, not a Yankee in sight or even a puff of smoke."

Huger's division was not withdrawn to their camps, which were on Gilliss creek, close to the east suburb of Richmond. This division was left well out on the Williamsburg road, in advance of D. H. Hill's intrenchments. On June 3 General Longstreet, for the information of General Lee, wrote: "The entire division of General Huger was left in advance upon retiring with the forces from the late battle-field. He was absent yesterday and not coming to report after being sent for, I ordered General Stuart to take the command of the division."[*]

The camps of the division under Whiting were on the Meadow Bridge road, north of Richmond. So far from returning to their camps, in the evening of June 1, as stated by Generals Johnston and Longstreet, this division remained closely confronting Sumner's corps at Fair Oaks Station for days after the battle ended.

---

[*] "Official Records," Vol. XI., Part III., p. 570.

At 3 A. M., June 2, the chief of General McClellan's staff wrote to General Heintzelman: "As General Sumner thinks he may be attacked at daylight, you will please hold your command ready to support him if necessary." And at the same hour, the following was sent to General Sumner: "The general commanding says in reply to your dispatch that you must do the best you can to hold your own if attacked. General Heintzelman will support you."

At 11.50 P. M., June 3, General Sumner wrote to General Kearney: "I have reason to expect a formidable attack to-morrow morning. Please advance with your division at 2 A. M. in order to attack the flank of the enemy if he assails me in large force. Everything may depend upon this movement of yours. Come directly up the railroad so as to arrive at Fair Oaks Station by daylight."

At 2.30 A. M., June 4, General Kearney ordered Colonel Ward, commanding Birney's brigade: "In compliance with within notice be ready to attack the enemy cautiously in flank toward Fair Oaks Station. Keep your own flank secure by a regiment thrown back at right angle to your advance." And at the same hour General Kearney ordered General Jameson: "In compliance with within be ready to move up the railroad, to cross and attack the enemy in flank if he does not attack you in front. Combine with Hobart Ward. Only commit two regiments."

The Federal advance on the Williamsburg road, June 2, is described by Lieutenant-Colonel H. L. Potter, Seventy-first New York. He says that with five companies he proceeded soon after dawn to re-occupy the position in the woods on the south side of the open ground around Casey's redoubt, from which he had, on the 1st, observed the Confederates until dark. He adds: "As we filed through the swamp the lines occupied by the enemy of the previous evening seemed to be abandoned. . . . From the wounded we learned that the enemy had fallen back that morning, commencing the retreat about midnight, and that their rear had not been an hour gone. . . . I continued to advance cautiously to the front . . . nearly one mile in front of the earthworks. . . . Halting in the edge of the wood looking out upon an open field for nearly half a mile in extent, we could see in the far front of the field some persons moving in the skirt of the wood. . . . I speedily returned to the line of earthworks, and sent . . . to report to General Sickles. Soon after General Hooker, commanding division, and General Sickles, with the Excelsior brigade, arrived in advance. . . . General Hooker desired me to accompany him to the front of the swamp to point out where the rebel cavalry had been seen. Just as we were returning a party of rebel skirmishers, who were concealed in the swamp, fired upon the general, killing one of the horses of his escort."

General Heintzelman says, that on the morning of the 2d of June, he "sent forward General Hooker with the portion of his division engaged the day before, to make a reconnaissance. . . . Our pickets got to within five miles of Richmond." Casey's skirmish line across the Williamsburg road, was but little more than five miles from Richmond when the Confederates advanced, May 31.

On the 2d of June, General Hooker reported to General Heintzelman: "I returned from my reconnaissance about 5 o'clock this P. M. . . . The enemy appeared to have a regiment of cavalry and three of infantry, but as the latter were most concealed in the forest, it was not prudent to determine their number; it may have been much greater. Our picket exchanged a few shots. On my return my command encamped in rear of Casey's camp."

The infantry posted "in the forest" were the three brigades of Huger's division. Under the circumstances General Hooker was right: "it was not prudent to determine their number."

On the Federal side there seems to have been a concurrence of views in favor of a "theory," which finds expression in the following quotations from "high authorities:"

General Barnard says: "The repulse of the rebels at Fair Oaks should have been taken advantage of. It was one of those occasions which, if not seized, do not repeat themselves. We now know the state of disorganization and dismay in which the rebel army retreated. We now know that it could have been followed into Richmond."

General Webb says: "The attempt of the rebels to drive the

[Federal] left wing into the Chickahominy, and cut McClellan's line of supply from White House, which opened with every prospect of success, was turned first into failure and then into disaster, which sent them to Richmond in a panic on the night of June 1."

General J. Watts De Peyster says: "At Fair Oaks or Seven Pines Kearney and Hooker could have gone into Richmond, supported by the bull-dog Sumner, if they had been permitted."

In short, the generally accepted "theory," on the Federal side, is: The Confederates, in full force, made a determined attack, June 1; were repulsed, retreated "to Richmond in a panic;" in "disorganization and dismay;" and might easily have been followed into that city.

The facts do not sustain this "theory" in a single particular. The Federals, in position, were attacked on the 1st of June by but two Confederate brigades; that attack was repulsed. Four Federal regiments then advanced and attacked a position held by one Confederate brigade; these four regiments were withdrawn from the front of that brigade. It is not necessary to refer again to the so called "bayonet charges" described by Generals Hooker and French.

On the 2d of June two Confederate divisions were quietly withdrawn to their former positions in front of Richmond. One division was left well out on the Williamsburg road, far in advance of the position held on that road by the Confederates previous to the attack; and one division, on the Nine-miles road, remained in position, closely confronting Sumner's corps, at Fair Oaks Station.

The official records show very clearly what Generals Sumner, Kearney and Hooker thought of the situation on the 2d, 3d and 4th of June.

The favored "theory," on the Confederate side, finds expression in the following quotation from the writings of General Richard Taylor. He says: "Johnston's plan was well considered and singularly favored of fortune. Some two corps of McClellan's army were posted on the southwest or Richmond side of the Chickahominy, and a sudden rise of that stream swept away the bridges and overflowed the adjacent low lands, cutting off those corps from their supports. They ought to have been crushed, but Johnston fell severely wounded, upon which confusion ensued, and no results of importance were attained."

This is an echo of General Johnston's claim, setting forth what would have been accomplished if he had not been disabled. That claim has already been referred to; and it is not proposed to discuss what General Taylor says on the subject.

The Chickahominy constituted an inherent disadvantage to the Federals in approaching Richmond from a base of operations on the Pamunkey river. This made it the more incumbent on General McClellan not to risk a corps unsupported, for several days, within easy reach of the Confederate army. But Keyes's corps was at Seven Pines, Heintzelman's at Bottom's Bridge and White Oak Bridge, whilst three Federal corps were on the north side of the Chickahominy. If Heintzelman's corps had been at the third line of defense, and Sumner's had crossed the river a day or two sooner, been placed on the Nine-miles road, west of Fair Oaks Station, and its position strengthened by fortifications, the Federals on the south side of the Chickahominy, May 31, would have been reasonably secure against attack. But, in the existing state of affairs, Keyes's corps was in imminent danger of destruction.

General Longstreet misunderstood the direction in which his own division was to have moved into action. Instead of striking Keyes's exposed, weak and easily accessible right flank, when D. H. Hill commenced the attack in front, Longstreet transferred his division to the Williamsburg and Charles City roads, allowed Hill to fight for three hours without any assistance, and then gave him one brigade. Hill sent that brigade to the point at which Longstreet's whole division should have been put in close action when the attack commenced. That brigade beat Keyes, whilst D. H. Hill's division was checked at the second abatis, and his right was forced back to the earthworks of Keyes's front line.

Five of the six brigades of Longstreet's division were not put in close action that day. Yet, General Longstreet attributed "the failure of complete success" to the "slow movements of General Huger's command"! General Johnston united with Longstreet in severely censuring Huger, and says: "The skill, vigor and decision with which these operations were conducted by General

Longstreet are worthy of the highest praise"! And he carefully suppressed the fact of Longstreet's "misunderstanding" and the failure of the attempt to have that misunderstanding corrected.

General Johnston's intention to concentrate a large portion of his army against the Federal force, isolated at Seven Pines, *was* well considered. But his written orders were unnecessarily delayed, and when issued were not of that clear and positive character called for by the occasion. His verbal instructions to General Longstreet were "misunderstood" by the latter; and the attempt to have that "misunderstanding" corrected failed, because of the capture of the Aide-de-Camp who bore the order. There is but little to commend in General Johnston's practical management of the army, May 31; and the same may be said in regard to the accounts he has given of these events.

General Longstreet, in command of the three divisions which were to have crushed Keyes's corps before it could be re-enforced, blundered badly from the beginning to the end of the battle; and, to say the least, his writings in reference to Seven Pines are no more creditable than his conduct of operations on the field.

It is not deemed necessary to dwell at more length upon what Generals Johnston and Longstreet say in regard to the causes which saved Keyes's corps from annihilation—and McClellan from decisive disaster—in the first great contest between the Federal Army of the Potomac and the Confederate Army of Northern Virginia.

Strength of the Opposing Armies.

McClellan's forces numbered 98,008[*] on the 31st of May, 1862, of which about 5,000 were on detached service. "Present for duty"—Sumner's corps, 17,412; Heintzelman's corps, 16,999; Keyes' corps, 17,132; Porter's corps, 17,546; Franklin's corps, 19,580; engineers, cavalry and provost guard, 4,767. Each corps was composed of two divisions of nearly equal strength.

General Johnston estimates the strength of his army at 73,928[†]. Other authorities place it at 62,696. The records show that on the 21st of May, 1862, ten days before the battle, Johnston's army numbered 53,688[‡].—Smith's division, 10,592; Long-

---

[*] "Official Records," Vol. XI., Part III., page 204.
[†] *Century Magazine*, May, 1885, page 114.
[‡] "Official Records," Vol. XI., Part III., page 530.

street's division, 13,816; Magruder's forces—composed of McLaws' division and D. R. Jones' division, 15,920; D. H. Hill's division, 11,151; cavalry and reserve artillery, 2,209.

Before May 31 Johnston's force was increased by the arrival of A. P. Hill's division (estimated) 4,000, and Huger's division (estimated) 5,008. One of the five brigades of D. H. Hill's division was detached before May 31.

In the three Union corps, that were engaged, the aggregate present for duty was 51,543.

In the four Confederate divisions, engaged, the aggregate present for duty was about 39,000.

Losses.

The total Union loss* was 790 killed, 3,594 wounded, and 647 captured or missing. Aggregate, 5,031.

The total Confederate loss† was 980 killed, 4,749 wounded, and 405 captured or missing. Aggregate, 6,134.

---

* "Official Records," Vol. XI., Part I., page 762.

† General Longstreet's report, "Official Records," Vol. XI., Part I., page 942, shows that the losses in the three divisions, which composed the "right wing" of General Johnston's army, were, 816 killed; 3,739 wounded; and 296 missing. The official report of the Chief Surgeon of the division under Whiting shows that the losses in that division, were, 164 killed; 1,010 wounded; and 109 missing. G. W. S.

Hd Qrs Harrison's
May 29th 1862

My dear General,

I have just received the note you wrote in regard to your Camp. I will give precise orders not to let it be interfered with. I received a message from Huger to the effect that his troops had not arrived at 6½ 7 o' this morning. No cars having been sent for them. The Qr Mr who had charge of the matter reported to me at sun set that the trains were ready — & would be off at 9 o.c. Lee ordered John G. Walker's brigade to Petersburg — & Holmes ordered it back.

For any purpose but that certain Matter yesterday the present disposition of our troops

troops is not good. Too strong on the extreme left. If nothing is heard of ~~heard~~ McDowell we must bring you back to a more central place.

D. H. Hill reported an hour ago that one of his advanced brigadiers had sent forward two-hundred skirmishers who very soon met a brigade of the enemy with cavalry & artillery. Who knows but that in the course of the morning Longstreet's scheme may accomplish itself.

If we get into a fight here you'll have to hurry to help us.

I think it will be best for A. P. H.'s troops to watch the bridges & for yours to be well in this direction — ready to act any where. Tell G. W.

Yours truly
J. E. Johnston

Brig. Gen. E. Whiting

Harrison's,
May 27th 1862

Gustavus,
 We must get ready to fight. Anderson (sundown 11 a.m.) reports, that his videttes have informed him that McDowell is advancing "in force" — his pickets at Juckers's. The army reported at six miles this' side of Fredericksburg.
 His main force at Half Sink — 3 regiments under Hamilton, at the junction. We must get ready for him.
 Yours ever
 J. E. Johnston

Major Genl Smith

Richmond
June 28th 1862.

My dear Gustavus,
                I enclose herewith the three first sheets of your report, to ask a modification — or omission rather.. They contain two subjects which I never intended to make generally known — & which I have mentioned to no one but yourself — I mentioned to you as I have been in the habit of doing every thing of interest in the Military way. I refer to the mention of the misunderstanding between Long-street & Myself in regard to the direction of his division, & that of his note to be received about & O.C. complaining of my slowness — which note I showed you.

                As it seems to me that both of these matters concern Longstreet & Myself alone, I have no hesitation in asking you to strike them out of of your report — as they in no manner concern your operations.

I received information of L's misunderstanding (which may be my fault, as I told you at the time) while his troops were moving to the Williamsburg road. I sent to L. to send 3 brigades by the Nine Mile road, if they had not marched so far as to make the change involve a serious loss of time — this after telling you of the misunderstanding.

Your march from your "Seven" H'dqr's was not in consequence of the letter from L. — Whiting had gone at my request with your specifications to ascertain the state of things with L. Just before 4. O.C. we heard musketry for the first time, & Whiting was ordered to advance — just then Major W. rode up & reported from L. & a moment after the note was brought me — which, after reading it, I forwarded to you.*

---

* The foregoing two pages are *fac-similes* of the first two pages of a letter addressed to me by General J. E. Johnston. The portions of that letter which are omitted make no mention of anything connected with the battle of Seven Pines. G. W. S.

Richmond 1st June '62
5 am

Genl

Your letter of this morn just recd. Ripley will be ordered & such forces from Genl Holmes as can be got up — will be sent — Your movements are judicious & determination to strike the enemy right — Try & ascertain his position & how he can best be hit —. I will send such Engineers as I can raise. But with Stevens Whiting Alexander &c what can I give you like them — You are right in calling upon me for what you want — I wish I could do more — It will be a glorious thing if you can gain a complete victory — Our success on the whole yesterday was good, but not complete —

Truly
R E Lee
Genl

Genl G. W. Smith
Commdg Army of N. Va.

Hd Qrs, June 1st 1862
S.O.C.

Major,
Yours of 6 is rec'd
I have ordered a brigade
of Gen Huger's as agreed
upon to the support of
Gen Whiting. Please
send a guide for it
Longstreet
Maj Whiting   Maj Gen

Hd'Qrs, June 1st 62

General

The Brigade cannot be spared. Every man except a Brigade is engaged in action. As you are not fighting I did not send it nor can I spare it. If I find myself at any time so that I spare it I will send it. But I am now not able to do without it.

J W Nrof

Gen Smith   D Longstreet

Major   June 1st

Yours of to day is received. The entire Army seems to be opposed to me. I trust that some diversion may be made in my favor during these successive attacks — Else my troops cannot stand it — The ammunition gives out too readily —

                        J E Johnston

Maj Milton   Maj Gen
                            Comg

Hd Qrs. 10. A m June 1st

General
Can you Re-enforce me, the entire army seems to be opposed to me. We cannot hold out unless we get help. If we can fight together, we can finish the work to-day, and Mc. time will be up. If I cant get help from that I must fall back.

Genl Smith   Longstreet

Genl Smith

I send a courier to bring Genl Cobbs Brigade Longstreet says he can hold his position with five thousand more men — He has now the same ground the enemy had yesterday, a drummer boy taken says that McClelland has gone to Washington to see after a man called Jackson

L de L,

Hd Qrs, June 1st 62
1½ P.M.

General.

I have just rec'd
a note from Maj. Milton
I will give instructions to
Gen Hill to extend his
line of Skirmishers to the
Rail road. The next attack
will be from Sumners
Division I think that
if we can whip it we
shall be comparatively
safe from the ~~army~~ advance
of McClellans Army —
I hope that those who

were whipped yesterday, will not appear again. The attack this morning was made at an unfortunate time. They had but little ammunition but we have since replenished our supply. And I sincerely hope that we may succeed against them in their next effort,

Oh that I had ten thousand men more

with Respects

Longstreet
Maj Gen
Comm—

Gen G W Smith
Comm'd
Our line is already
connected Gen Stuart says
by Cavalry Videttes.
JL

MAPS.

I am indebted to the Century Magazine Company for permission to use duplicates of the plates of the two maps which were first published in "Battles and Leaders of the Civil War." These are believed to be, by far, the most accurate maps of this battle. But there are a few unimportant errors in minor details; caused, no doubt, by the fact that too much was attempted to be shown. The pentangular redoubt is placed too far south of the road—the first abatis was wider than indicated, and extended south so as to cover the whole front of Casey's main line—the ground on the south and east of Seven Pines was open for 300 or 400 yards from that point—the ground near the positions marked for Pickett's and Armistead's brigades, going into action, was not open—the regiments that supported Spratt's battery were not all in Naglee's brigade. Hood's brigade, at 5 P. M., was very near Fair Oaks Station.

But, these minor matters detract but little from the general correctness of the maps. In all cases of discrepancy between the maps and the text, the latter should control, because it is based on the official reports of those subordinate commanders whose troops did the actual fighting.

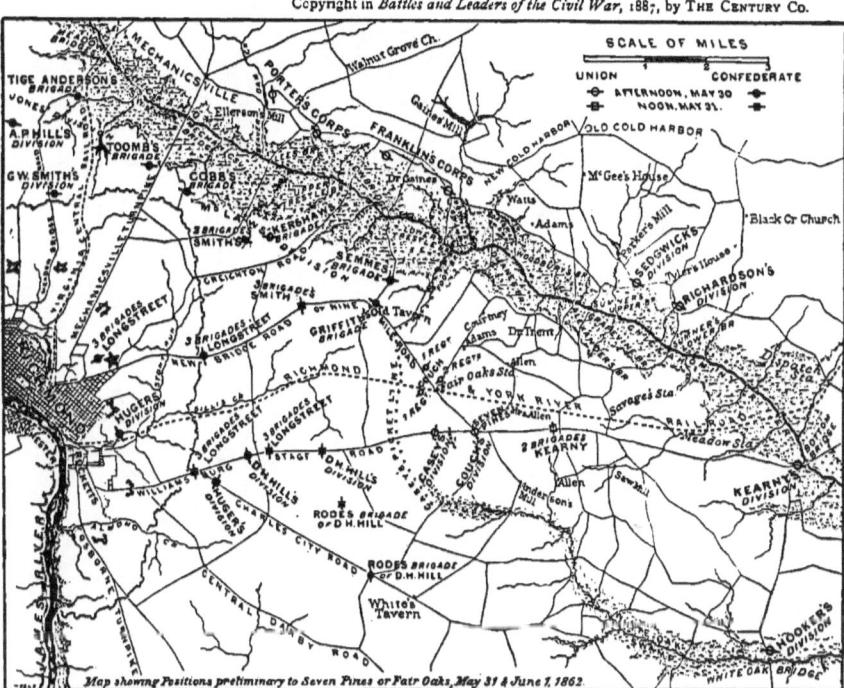

MAP SHOWING POSITIONS PRELIMINARY TO THE BATTLE OF SEVEN PINES.

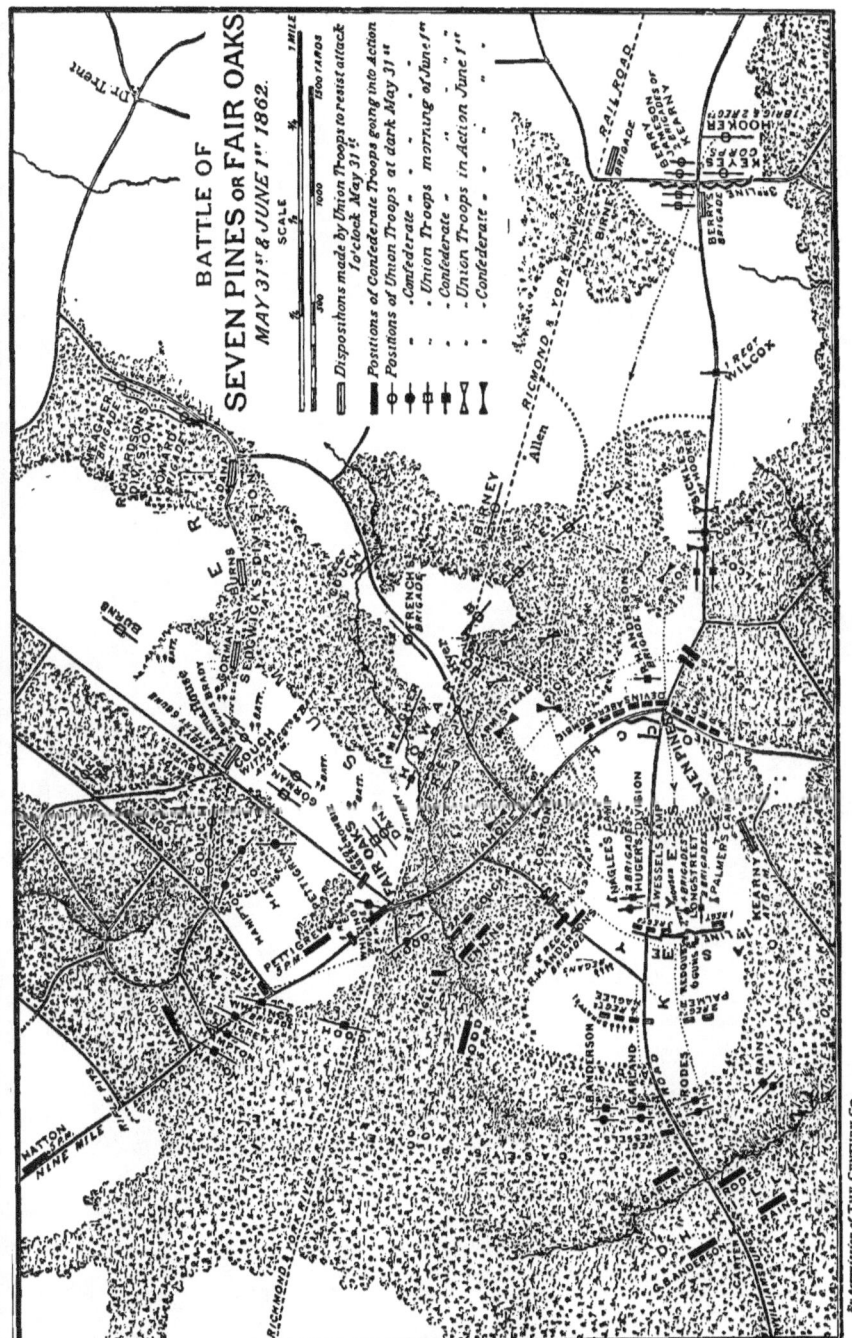

INDEX.

	PAGE.
Abatis, or felled timber	28-9, 188
Abercrombie, Brigadier-General J. J.	39, 46, 85-8
Accounts given by "historians," conflicting ; see Preface, and "Theories"	169-70
Adams's house	115, 120
Anderson, Colonel G. B.	47-9, 52-5
Anderson, Colonel G. T.	10, 15
Anderson, Brigadier-General R. H.	52-9
Anderson, Major William	61
Archer, Colonel J. J	96, 132
Armistead, Brigadier-General L. A.	79, 120-1-2-3, 140, 141, 159
Army of Northern Virginia, organization of	7, 8
Position of	12
Strength of	7, 16, 172
Losses of	173
Army of the Potomac, organization of	28, 172
Position of	28, 171
Strength of	7, 172
Losses of	173
Attack, May 31, signal given and movement described	47
June 1, described	119, 123, 140
Baird, Major W. H., extracts from official report of, Thirty-eighth New York	110
Barlow, Colonel F. C., extracts from official report of, Sixty-first New York	112
Barnard, Brigadier-General J. G.	157, 169
Bayonet-charges ; " so-called " ; French	114-15, 160-61
Hooker	116-17-18, 159-60
Beauregard, General G. T.	70
Beaverdam Creek	10, 11, 14
Beckham, Captain R. F., Aide	21, 24, 25
Berry, Brigadier-General H. G.	41-2-4-6
Birney, Brigadier-General D. B.	41-4, 84-6, 105-6-7, 110-11-12-15
Blanchard, Brigadier-General A. G.	79
Bondurant's battery	49
Bottom's Bridge	12, 28, 41-2-7, 157, 171
Brady's battery	84-5-7, 105
Bratton, Colonel John	59, 60-3
Briggs, Colonel H. S.	40-1
Brooke, Colonel J. R.	109, 112 13

	PAGE.
Burns, Brigadier-General W. W	86-8, 93, 110
Cameron, Governor W. E	31, 120
Carpenter, Captain J. Q	69
Carter's battery	49, 50-2
Casey, Brigadier-General Silas	28
Extracts from official report of	34-5
Cruel injustice to	36
Chickahominy, described	9
Cobb, Brigadier-General Howell	10, 128, 137
Cochrane, Colonel John, extracts from official report of, Sixty-fifth New York	88
Colston, Brigadier-General R. E	31, 56, 79
Correspondence, with General Johnston, in reference to his "original plan"	16, 17, 18
With General D. H. Hill, in reference to Longstreet's letter of June 7, 1862	66-67
With Longstreet on the field, June 1	134-5-7-8
Couch, Brigadier-General D. N	28-39
Extracts from official report of	40-84
Court, applied for by General Huger	74
Not granted	76
Cross, Colonel E E., extracts from official report of, Fifth New Hampshire	114
Dana, Brigadier-General N. J. T	86, 91
Extracts from official report of	92
Davis, President Jefferson, dissatisfied	9
Rides out to see the action commence	10
Practical refusal to grant Huger's request for a court	76
Makes "some explanation"	77
Efforts to send a brigade "to attack the enemy in flank and reverse"	101-2
Asks for plans	103
Ordered General R. E. Lee to take command	137
Davis, Colonel W. W. H., extracts from official report of, One Hundred and Fourth Pennsylvania	36-7
Dearing's battery	52
De Peyster, General J. Watts	170
Devens, Brigadier-General Charles, extracts from official report of	40
Egan, Lieutenant-Colonel T. W., extracts from official report of, Fortieth New York	111, 115
Fac-similes, notes and letters	174 to 187
Frank, Colonel Paul	109
Frank's battery	106
French, Brigadier-General W. H	105-6
Extracts from official report of	108-9, 160
French, Major S. B	24-5-6
Frobel, Colonel B. W	26-7, 97-8

INDEX.

	PAGE.
Gap between Longstreet's left and Whiting's right............129, 132, 164	
Garland, Brigadier-General Samuel..............................47-8-9, 55	
Gordon, Colonel J. B., extracts from official report of..................	54-5
Gorman, Brigadier-General W. A., extracts from official report of 89, 90	
Griffith, Brigadier-General Richard..................................99, 102	
Hampton, Brigadier-General Wade.....................7, 22, 98-9, 100-1, 133	
Hatton, Brigadier-General Robert......................7, 22, 98-9, 100-1, 133	
Hazzard, Captain G. W., batteries ; extracts from official report of....106, 110	
Heintzelman, Brigadier-General S. P..28, 41-2-3-6-47, 63-4, 139, 168-9, 171-2	
Hill, Major-General A. P 8, 9, 13, 15, 16, 23, 128-9, 130-3, 172	
Hill, Major-General D. H.................	7, 8
Directed by Longstreet to move at dawn, but "not to move until relieved by Huger's division ".............	148
Inevitable delay caused by that order	148
Moved at 1 P. M...	47
Fighting for possession of the Federal first line of defense.......	47–52
Asked Longstreet for an additional brigade................	52
Fighting for possession of the Federal second line of defense..52 to 63	
Position of the division, night of May 31...................... ..	55–6
Thirteen brigades under his orders, June 1....................139, 140	
Official report of operations on the 1st of June..............139 to 142	
Received no orders from Longstreet the second day.............	140
Ordered, after dark, to withdraw......	142
Comments on Longstreet's letter of June 7, 1862................	66-7
Hood, Brigadier-General J. B...7, 10, 22, 94-5-6-7-8-9, 123, 127, 132-3, 162-3	
Hooker, Brigadier-General Joseph 20, 46	
Extracts from official report of.......... ....115, 116	
Additional mention 117-8, 157-9, 160, 169, 170	
Howard, Aide, C. H...	114
Howard, Brigadier-General O. O................................	105
Extracts from official report of...............................	106-9
Additional mention........................... 112-14-15	
Hudson, Lieutenant-Colonel H. W., extracts from official report of, Eighty-seventh New York...............................	90
Huger, Captain Benjamin.....................................	118
Huger, Major-General Benjamin, in camp on Gilliss Creek.............	16
Ordered to move out on Charles City road.....................	67-8
Delayed at the crossing of Gilliss Creek by Longstreet's division.81-2, 72	
Under Longstreet's orders after 10 or 11 A. M.	32, 74
Two brigades of Huger's division placed in rear of three brigades of Longstreet's division, by Longstreet's order..............	79
Charged with slowness by Generals Longstreet and Johnston..64-5-9, 70	
Objects to Longstreet's report..........................	72
Objects to Johnston's indorsement of Longstreet's " erroneous statements "...	73
Applies for a court	74
Court not granted...............................	76

INDEX.

	PAGE.
Huger, Major-General Benjamin—	
Johnston's letter on the subject..................	75
General Johnston sided with Longstreet against Huger........	68
Longstreet ordered General Stuart to take command of Huger's division..	167
Hunt, Captain L. C., Aide...................................	41
Jameson, Brigadier-General C. D.............................	42-4-5-6
Jenkins, Colonel Micah......................................	52-8
Extracts from official report of........................	59 to 63
Johnson, Lieutenant-Colonel C. F., extracts from official report of, Eighty-first Pennsylvania.............................	109
Johnston, General J. E., commanded the Army of Northern Virginia...	7
Awaited the closer approach of the Federals, east of Richmond...	12, 15, 144 5
Attention suddenly called to the right of the Federal army......	12, 13
Preparations for attack in that direction...................	13, 14
Movement suspended	14, 15
Letter to General Whiting, commanding G. W. Smith's division..	8, 9
When attack was determined upon it had not commenced to rain.	146
Written order for movement of division under Whiting.........	18
Written order for movement of Huger's division.............	67-8
Longstreet " was instructed verbally ".....................	28
Correspondence in regard to "original plan"...............	16, 17, 18
Intention at sunrise on the 31st of May..................	20-1-2, 145-6
Elated at the prospect of striking an effective blow............	147
Expectations would have been better founded if his orders had been given sooner......................................	147-8
Letter in reference to Longstreet's "misunderstanding"........	19, 20
Aide captured...	25, 34
Anxiety because of Longstreet's delay.....................	22-6
Received a note from Longstreet complaining of "slowness" on the Nine-miles road..................................	19
Directed the division under Whiting "against the right flank of Longstreet's adversaries "..............................	94
Censured Whiting for hesitating to move the division across the railroad...	97
"Obstinately thought" there was only one Federal brigade in position north of Fair Oaks Station..........................	95
Disabled by wounds and removed from the field..............	154
Sided with Longstreet against Huger......................	68
Letter to Confederate Secretary of War, in reference to Huger...	75
Praises Longstreet......................................	171
Statement of the positions of the contending forces on the night of May 31 and morning of June 1........................	153-4-5
Amazed "at the swelling bulk assumed by the 'skirmish' of the 1st"...	159

INDEX.

Johnston, General J. E.—
    Says General Smith "was prevented from renewing his attack"...... 155
    Claims that three Federal corps would have been destroyed on the
        1st of June if he had not been disabled on the 31st of May.155 to 158
    Longstreet's "misunderstanding," May 31, "may have been"
        Johnston's "fault"..151, 152

Jones, Brigadier-General D. R..8, 13, 128
Kearney, Brigadier-General Philip.. 28
    Extracts from official report of.. 44–5
    Additional mention..................................46, 107, 168, 170
Kemper, Brigadier-General J. L.................................24, 52-3-6-7
Kershaw, Brigadier-General J. B.. 128
Keyes, Brigadier-General E. D.. 28
    Reported his condition.. 29
    Speaks more in detail.. 29
    Extracts from official report of...............37, 39, 40, 42, 43, 45, 46
    Additional mention........47, 83-4-5, 101, 139, 146, 147, 154, 157, 171
Kimball, Colonel J. W., extracts from official report of, Fifteenth
    Massachusetts... 91
Kirby, Lieutenant Edmund, battery.. 86
    Extracts from official report of.. 87
Langley, Lieutenant-Colonel S. G.. 114
Law, Colonel E. M.. 95
Lee, General R. E..9, 10, 101-2-4
    Letter to General G. W. Smith.. 130
    Additional mention..............................131-7-8-9, 165-6-7
Lee, Colonel S. D.. 100
Lee, Colonel W. R., extracts from official report of, Twentieth Massachu-
    setts.. 92
Lemmon, Captain George, Aide...95-6, 132
Lightfoot, Colonel C. E.. 100
Lomax, Colonel Tennent..119-20-21
Longstreet, Major-General James... 7, 8
    Proposed that an attack be made, May 29th............................ 15
    Was to precede Whiting.. 19
    "Misunderstanding".. 19, 20
    May have been Johnston's "fault"..................................151, 152
    Delayed Whiting..19, 21, 24, 25
    Delayed Huger..31, 72
    Order he gave D. H. Hill caused delay.................................. 148
    Additional delay caused by "mismanagement"...................148-9,150
    Claimed to rank and to command Huger.............................32, 76
    Held three brigades of his own division and two brigades of
        Huger's division on Charles City road............................79, 80
    Five brigades of his own division were not in close action the
        first day..32, 33, 63, 66, 71, 81, 154
    Complained of General Johnston's "slowness".......................... 19

Longstreet, Major-General James—
    Effect of that complaint..22, 149
    Complained of Huger's "slow movements".................. 65
    Was ordered to renew the attack June 1st...................... 131
    Failed to obey that order................................. 140, 166
    Battle-field notes.............................134, 135, 137, 138
    Recollection of the fighting the second day................... 163
    Description of what occurred after General Lee took command.165, 166
    Ordered General Stuart to take command of Huger's division.... 167
Losses, May 31, Confederate: D. H. Hill's division.................. 63
    Longstreet's division 56, 63
    G. W. Smith's division, under Whiting....................... 101
Losses, May 31, Federal: Casey's division...................... 46
    Couch's division.. 46
    Kearney's division.. 46
    Sedgwick's division and Couch's "cut off" forces 93
Losses, June 1, Confederate: Mahone's brigade................... 121
    Pickett's brigade.. 126
    Wilcox's brigade... 118
    Hood's brigade... 132
    Tomlin's regiment.. 122
    Armistead's brigade referred to 141
    Pryor's brigade referred to.................................. 118
Losses, June 1, Federal: Richardson's division..................... 115
    Hooker's division.. 116
    Birney's brigade... 115
Losses, aggregate, in the two days: Army of Northern Virginia....... 173
    Army of the Potomac... 173

McClellan, Major-General G. B., commanded the army of the Potomac.. 7
    Positions occupied on the 30th of May........................ 28
    Telegram to Secretary Stanton, June 1 .... 35, 36
    Ordered General Sumner to cross the Chickahominy............ 83
    Risked an isolated corps in vicinity of Seven Pines.............. 171
    Ordered Heintzelman to hold his command ready to assist Sumner 168
McDowell, Major-General Irvin, moved from Fredericksburg toward
        Richmond.. 12, 13
    Returned 14
    Moved north... 14
    Additional mention....................................... 8, 144
McLaws, Major-General Lafayette................................. 8
    Reported advance of Federal skirmishers...................... 12
    To "re-enforce Longstreet".................................. 18
    Reported the Federals were constructing a pontoon bridge....... 128
    The location of each brigade of his division 128
    Bearer of message and orders to General Longstreet 136
    His note in reference to General Longstreet.................... 137

Smith, Major-General G. W.—
    Repaired to General Johnston's headquarters.................. 20
    Official report of what occurred there....................... 20-1-2
    Report of the fighting in the woods north of Fair Oaks Station..98, 99, 100
    Circumstances under which that report was written............ 27-8
    General Johnston requested certain portions of that report should
        be omitted.. 19
    Correspondence in reference to General Johnston's "original
        plan"... 17, 18
    Ordered General Longstreet to renew the attack on the 1st of June. 131
    Correspondence with General Longstreet on the 1st of June... 134-5-7-8
    Gave up the command of the army to General Lee.............. 137
    Correspondence with General D. H. Hill...................... 66, 139
    Interview with President Davis, at dark, on the 31st of May..... 103
    Extracts from official report of operations on the 1st of June.... 130
Spratt's battery...34-5-6
Staples, Colonel H. A., extracts from official report of, Third Maine.... 111
Stevens, Major W. H.. 132-5
Strength of the opposing armies..................................... 172-3
Stribling's battery.. 142
Stuart, Brigadier-General J. E. B.........................127-8, 134-8, 167
Suiter, Colonel J. A., extracts from official report of, Thirty-fourth New
    York.. 90
Sully, Colonel Alfred, extracts from official report of, First Minnesota.. 88
Sumner, Brigadier-General E. V..................................... 28
    Ordered to cross the Chickahominy............................ 83
    Extracts from official report of 83-4
    Found Couch's troops "in line near Adams's house"............ 84
    Sedgwick's division, four regiments of Couch's division, and two
        batteries resist attack.................................. 84 to 89
    Ordered five regiments to charge against Whiting's right........ 124-7
    Placed Richardson's division along the railroad................. 105
    Fighting on Richardson's line.............................105 to 115
    Expected "a formidable attack" on the 4th of June............. 168
Suydam, Captain C. C., Aide... 85
Swinton's History 17, 18, 23, 26, 27, 159
Taylor, General Richard 170, 171
"Theories," Confederate.. 170
    Federal 169, 170
Tomlin, Colonel H. B., extracts from official report of, Fifty-third
    Virginia...121, 122
Trophies, Confederate 142
Van Ness, Captain W. W... 84
Waddill, Major G. M..121, 122
Walker, Colonel Elijah, extracts from official report of, Fourth Maine.. 112
Walker, Brigadier-General J. G 8

INDEX.

	PAGE.
Ward, Colonel J. H. H., extracts from official report of	107
Ordered three regiments to charge	110
Washington, Lieutenant J. B., Aide to General Johnston	21, 25, 34
Watson's battery	142
Webb, Major-General A. S	169, 170
Wessells, Brigadier-General H. W., extracts from official report of	26
Whiting, Major Jasper	20, 131-2-4

Whiting, Brigadier-General W. H. C., assigned to command G. W. Smith's division 7
    Instructions from General Johnston 8, 9
    Ordered by General Johnston to move to a point on the Nine-miles road 18
    Delayed by Longstreet's division 19, 21, 24, 25
    Attacks Federal re-enforcements 83, 93-101
    Position just after dark on the 31st of May 127
    Ordered to make a diversion in favor of the real attack Longstreet was ordered to make on the 1st of June 131, 133
    Ordered to throw back his right 134
    Closely confronted Sumner's corps 143, 167

Wilcox, Brigadier-General C. M., position and command on the 30th of May 30
    Moved to the junction of the Williamsburg and Charles City roads 31
    Marched and countermarched on the Charles City road under Longstreet's orders 79
    Three companies of these three brigades in close action on the 31st of May 56-7
    Operations of his brigade and Pryor's on the 1st of June 117, 118

Williams, Colonel D. H., extracts from official report of, Thirty-first Pennsylvania 89

Withdrawal, from the captured works 142-3, 166-7
    Discovered by the Federals 168-9

INDEX.   199

	PAGE.
Magruder, Major-General J. B., commanded the "centre" of the army of Northern Virginia	8
Additional mention	13, 95, 99, 101, 102
Mahone, Brigadier-General William, moved on the Charles City road	31
Ordered to Seven Pines	119
Ordered to attack	118
Two of his regiments were on detached service	119
Describes the fighting done by the three other regiments	119, 120
Maps; memoranda in reference to	188
Maurin's battery	142
Meagher, Brigadier-General T. F	105, 110
Mindil, Brigadier-General G. W	152, 163
Miller, Colonel James	109
Moore, Colonel Sydenham	56

Naglee, Brigadier-General H. M., position and strength of brigade..... 36
Extracts from official report of........................ 37-8-9, 42-3
Neill, Colonel T. H... 39, 40
Nevin, Lieutenant-Colonel D. J., extracts from official report of, Sixty-
    second New York 86

Organization 7, 8, 28, 172-3

Palmer, Brigadier-General I. N., extracts from official report of........ 36
Parker, Colonel T. T , extracts from official report of, Sixty-fourth New
    York.. 113
Peck, Brigadier-General J. J., position................................. 39
    Mention..43-5-6
Pender, Colonel W. D.. 98
Pettigrew, Brigadier-General J. J.............. 7, 12, 22, 94-8-9, 100, 101
Pettit's battery..106-7, 110
Pickett, Captain Charles... 125
Pickett, Brigadier-General G. E., extracts from official report of........ 92
    Ordered to attack 123
    Describes his movement.. 123
    "From having been the attacking party," "had to act on the
        defensive"... 124
    Describes the fighting... 125
    Re-enforced by Colston and Mahone................................. 125
    Complained that he was not aided by "the left wing of our
        army"... 162
    Covered the withdrawal of the right wing on the morning of the
        2d of June 107
Pitcher, Captain W. L.. 112
Positions of the contending forces—
    On the night of May 30: Confederates........................16, 145
        Federals..28, 146

200   INDEX.

Positions of the contending forces—
    On the night of May 31 and morning of June 1: Confederates ... 55–6–7, 62, 127, 136, 155–6
        Federals..46–7, 105–6, 156–7
    On the night of June 1 and morning of June 2—Confederates.... 167
        Federals.. 168–9
Potter, Lieutenant-Colonel H. L., describes Federal movements when it was discovered the Confederates had withdrawn from the captured works... 168–9
Pryor, Brigadier-General R. A..............................79, 117, 118

Rains, Brigadier-General G. T................................... 47
    Declined to come up.. 49
    Ordered by General Hill "to make a wide flank movement"...... 50
    Report of... 51
    Failed to support Rodes's right................................ 53
    Position night of May 31....................................... 56
Richardson, Brigadier-General I. B.............................. 28
    Extracts from official report of................................ 105
    Position of his lines... 105–6
    First firing about 5 A. M...................................... 107
    Heavy attack 6.30 A. M.. 108
    Ordered General Howard to re-enforce the first line........... 108
Riker, Colonel J. L... 86
Ripley, Brigadier-General R. S............................... 130–6
Rippey, Colonel O. H... 39, 40
Rodes, Brigadier-General R. E................................ 30, 47
    Ordered to Williamsburg road.................................. 71
    Extracts from official report of............................. 49, 53
    Ordered to dislodge the enemy in the woods south of the Williamsburg road.. 53
    The right of his brigade repulsed.............................. 53
    Position night of 31st of May.................................. 55
Russell, Colonel D. A.............................. 39, 85–6, 107, 110

Sands, Captain R. M.. 121
Sedgwick, Brigadier-General John............................... 28
    Extracts from official report of........................... 84, 85–6
    Mention.. 92, 105
Semmes, Brigadier-General P. J............................. 20, 128
Seven Pines, description of the ground and the defenses...... 28, 29
Sickles, Brigadier-General D. E............................. 116, 169
Sloan, Captain Benjamin, on Huger's staff...................... 32
Smith, Major-General G. W..................................... 7, 8
    The division which bore his name was commanded by General Whiting.. 8, 20
    Turned over the command of the left wing temporarily to A. P. Hill... 23